A WOMAN'S GUIDE TO
Healing the Heartbreak of Divorce

A Woman's Guide to

Healing
the Heartbreak
of Divorce

ROSE SWEET

HENDRICKSON
PUBLISHERS

Copyright © 2001 by Rose Sweet
Published by Hendrickson Publishers
P.O. Box 3473
Peabody, Massachusetts, 01961-3473

Printed in the United States of America

ISBN 1-56563-626-0

Third printing ---- September, 2002

Cover design by Richmond & Williams, Nashville, Tennessee
Interior design and typesetting by Reider Publishing Services,
   San Francisco, California
Edited by Judy Bodmer, Gwen Waller, and Deneen Sedlack

Library of Congress Cataloging-in-Publication Data
Sweet, Rose, 1951–
     A woman's guide to—healing the heartbreak of divorce /
Rose Sweet.
     p. cm.
     ISBN 1-56563-626-0 (paper)
     1. Divorce—Religious aspects—Christianity. 2. Divorced
women—Religious life. 3. Divorce—Psychological aspects. I. Title:
Healing the heartbreak of divorce. II. Title.
BT707 .S94 2001
248.8'433—dcsa   2001016821

To the men I married.

*God used my time with you, and the love we had,
to help build my character, and ultimately
to bring me closer to Him.*

For those blessings, and for you, I am thankful.

Table of Contents

Section II
Examining the Principles

Section III
Establishing New Priorities

Section IV
Empowering New Practices

Section V
Enjoying Your Passions

Acknowledgment

J never could have written this book without the love, encouragement, and prayers of many people. With deepest gratitude I especially want to thank:

Fred and Florence Littauer, my mentors and friends, who opened their hearts and home to me, providing constant love and acceptance before, during, and after my divorce;

Dr. Gary Lawrence, my Melancholy friend and Choleric counselor, who gave me practical tools to solve mental and emotional problems;

Dan Penwell, editor and Hendrickson's trade product manager, who believed I had something of value to say to readers, and who worked hard to perfect and polish the final product;

Judy Bodmer, Gwen Waller, and Deneen Sedlack, excellent editors who, clearly and kindly, sharpened my pencil with their red pens;

The CLASS (Christian Leaders, Authors & Speakers Services) staff, who work tirelessly to bring speakers and authors together with just the right publisher;

The men and women in DivorceCare who allowed me to use their stories to help others who are hurt, angry, or discouraged about their own divorce;

My parents and parochial school teachers who all taught me first, to love God, and second, to love reading and writing; and, finally,

My girlfriends, Ronda, Tammy, Ann, Lani, and Kristi, who *listened* . . . and kept me well-supplied with lots of shopping, lunches, and love.

Thank you all.

Foreword

When I first met Rose years ago, she was miserable in her marriage, but struggling bravely to do the right thing. I remember her telling me, "Florence, I want to stay, but at the same time I want to run away." Isn't that what we all feel at one time or another in our marriages?

Sometimes we make that fateful decision, and sometimes our spouse makes it for us. Either way, the pain and heartache of a failed relationship is devastating. Most women either stay stuck in their pain for years, or they shove it all inside and quickly move on to what they hope will be a new and happier life. Both responses are extremes, and neither will result in the peace every woman seeks.

Like a broken bone, the emotional wounds of divorce need to be x-rayed, reset, and given time to heal properly. The patient has to learn a new routine and is given permission to stay off her feet for awhile. It doesn't matter if you are dealing with new wounds or old scars, Rose gives you the prescription to healing *your* heartbreak.

This book is not just for recently divorced women. Any woman who is thinking of divorce, has a daughter, sister, or friend facing divorce, or who has moved on past a long-forgotten divorce, will appreciate this book. No matter what you have had to endure in your marriage or divorce, you can grow in grace, wisdom, and contentment. I know you will be comforted and encouraged by Rose's stories and those of the men and women she's counseled.

Rose writes from her heart . . . so that you can heal yours.

Florence Littauer
Author, *Personality Plus*

The Scarlet "D"

*T*he short, gray-haired man in the stylish silk suit approached my book table after a seminar in which I had disclosed my history of divorce. He waited patiently while the crowd offered me the usual compliments, bought books, and shared their own stories with me. Smiling, he then asked loudly, "So, you've been divorced *three* times?" With a sneer he added, "Didn't you *learn anything?*" All eyes were on me as he stood there self-righteously waiting for my answer.

For a split second I had the unholy thought of decking him, but my professional training kicked in and I gave him a small, polite nod. I was not afraid to share the truth. "No . . . as a matter of fact, I *didn't* learn."

I paused and watched his face fall because he'd failed in his thinly veiled attempt to shame me. Then I continued in a friendly tone, "I'm really glad you asked that question. After a divorce, many of us think we only need to deal with our grief and move on, which is exactly what I did. I had no idea that I needed to learn why I was making such poor choices. I had no one to teach me." I leaned toward him, reached out, and touched his sleeve lightly, adding with a genuine smile and an upbeat tone, "Thank goodness it's never too late to learn!"

He turned and walked away without saying another word. Whew! I had survived another subtle attack by a man I'm sure had been married fifty years, blissfully of course, who saw me as some kind of social misfit. I reminded myself that he was just one of millions of human beings, flawed like me and the rest of the world, but who didn't have to wear the big red "D" on *his* chest.

The Heartbreak of Divorce

My first marriage lasted only a few months. I was twenty and anxious to move out, away from my controlling mother and a houseful of seven younger siblings. Since I had no job skills and our family could not afford college, marriage seemed the only option. But when my new husband came home drunk (again) one night and hit me, I called my dad to come get me. My spouse refused to get counseling, and we were divorced shortly thereafter.

I was devastated. For years I was deeply depressed and distrusting, but everyone, including my family and friends, told me to move on. "You're young, you'll get over it," they said. I prayed and asked God to help me, and I tried to continue being a good person. Eventually I got over the outward pain, but I had no idea I still carried mental and emotional scars and lacked relationship skills.

When I hit my thirties and my biological clock was ticking loudly, I married mostly out of a desperation to have the family of which I'd always dreamed. Though ill-prepared and uneducated about ourselves and each other, my husband and I thought we had what it took. In reality, neither of us had any idea what we were doing. Despite our good intentions, after a few short years the marriage crumbled and I wanted out. I found myself again with no children, no family of my own, and the stigma of a second divorce.

I refused to enter my forties as a spinster. The compulsive need for marriage, children, and a real family pounded in my head day and night. Haunted by the realization something might be wrong with *me*, I went to counseling and returned to my knees asking God for his help. I learned a lot about dysfunction, relationship dynamics, and how my less-than-perfect childhood had affected me, but I still had miles to go before I was ready for marriage the way God intended.

My last husband came with an adorable two-year-old son, and I just couldn't resist the ready-made family package. Within a short time, however, I realized I had made another poor choice and that I needed help—big time. I begged God to forgive me for trying to direct my own life all these years and for trying to create the life I wanted instead of waiting to see what he wanted for me. Although I'd been a Christian since I was a young girl, I had never completely surrendered my will to his, but now I did, hoping it would save my third marriage. I started attending church on a more regular basis and teaching the children's Bible class. I devoted my entire life to praying, reading, learning, and absorbing all I could from twelve-step programs, marriage enrichment courses, and godly counselors. I listened to tapes, went to seminars, and memorized scripture. As God worked in my heart and healed my emotions, I finally started to become the woman he wanted me to be.

But it was too late for my marriage. After nearly ten years, my husband left one day to go find himself, and I couldn't stop him. Even though I was working on being the best spouse I could be, I couldn't control my husband's choices.

A successful marriage takes two mature people, or two people willing to work toward maturity. In my own middle-aged naiveté, I thought maturity was being over twenty-one, having a college education, owning a home, and holding a job. Like so many women, I thought if we both loved God and tried to be good, the rest would fall into place with relatively few problems. There's nothing like a divorce to make a woman realize how important it is to date prudently and for both parties to slowly and carefully prepare for marriage.

A Doctor in the House

In the years following my third divorce, I've facilitated an ongoing DivorceCare group at my church and participated with other group leaders throughout the world. DivorceCare, a resource from Church Initiative, is an international ministry based in North Carolina. The program equips churches of all denominations to help hurting people in all stages of separation or divorce. Through my writing and speaking ministry, I've counseled thousands of divorced men and women. Their stories, many of which are in this book by permission, are all different, but also the same. Whether we've been divorced for forty days or forty years, we're all hurting and we all need healing.

Fortunately the Master Physician is in the house. He'll show up with his little black bag any time, day or night, if only we give him a call. If you have any doubt that Jesus can bind your emotional wounds, take another look at the stories in the New Testament. Jesus healed the multitudes, including:

- The lepers (Mark 1:40–42; Luke 17:12–14)—The lepers were rejected by society, just as we are by our ex-spouses, friends, family, and sometimes even the church.
- Peter's mother-in-law (Mark 1:29–31)—Some of us are plagued by a "fever" of loneliness and frustration.
- The dead (Luke 7:12–15; 8:49–55; John 11:38–44)—Some fall into the "death" of depression and need to be raised back to life.
- The woman who bled (Matt. 9:20–22)—We may be stuck in unending grief like the woman who bled for years, and depleted by our financial, emotional, and physical losses.
- The blind (Matt. 9:27–30; 30:30–34; Mark 8:22–25)—Women who quickly bury themselves in their work or children can remain "blind" to their pain and the need for deeper levels of healing.
- The paralyzed and those suffering seizures (Matt. 9:2–7; 17:14–18)— All of us can be "paralyzed" by worry, have "seizures" of fear, and be so bitter and angry that we seem "demon-possessed!"

As we seek healing, we must remember that God made us flesh and bone, mind and emotions, and a spirit. We have spiritual, mental, emotional, physical, sexual, financial, material, and familial needs. And God cares about each one.

So how does God want us to handle the terrible tragedy of divorce? As he said long ago, he says to us today, "Come, follow me" (Matt. 4:19).

SECTION

I

Embracing the Pain

Love Letter

My Precious One,

Did you know I have watched you and loved you since before you were born? I know everything about you including your thoughts and your fears. I hear the beating of your broken heart. Before you even tell me what has hurt you, I know it. This divorce has ripped you open, and at times the misery is unbearable.

Even though you may not feel like I am here, or that I care, I want to assure you that I have my hand upon you. I love you more than you could ever imagine. If you will give me all your pain, your fears, and your entire life, I promise I will not only heal you, but I will give you the desires of your heart. Take my hand. Let me hold you close and love you the way you always have needed to be loved.

Your Loving Father

1

God Our Caring Parent

I'll never forget Tom's eyes.

The day my ex-husband left we had another one of those discussions that frequently occur in marriages in which one partner pursues and the other distances. Tired of arguing, I asked the generic question I knew would bring us back to the same page and wind things up.

"C'mon, honey, this is ridiculous. I know we can work this out. After all, we're both in this for life, right?" I'd asked this question a million times, and I knew what he'd say. His shoulders would relax, he'd give me a warm look, we'd hug, and we'd make up. Instead, he didn't answer.

I waited for what seemed like forever and then repeated, "For life, right?"

He looked straight through me with those green eyes that normally sparkled, but which now were dark and cold, and said flatly, "No."

I panicked. "What?" I thought maybe he was just trying to scare me. "What are you saying? That you don't want to be married?"

Still staring at me, his jaw set squarely and his white smile gone, he repeated that one word, "No."

My throat tightened and my stomach knotted as I heard the clear, simple truth in his voice. Tom got up and walked away, and within minutes he was out the door.

Shocked and scared, I paced frantically around the house and then threw myself on our bed. I didn't know what to think. Part of me was gone. I felt like someone had just shot a cannon ball through me, blowing a huge hole where my heart had been.

Do you remember the day your marriage ended? It doesn't really matter if you left him after years of frustration and broken promises, or if your husband left you. Most of us feel some relief to be away from the nightmare we called marriage, but we also experience the big black hole. That's why we need help.

In choosing to read this book, you've taken a giant step forward in your own healing process. Congratulations for knowing that help can come in many forms! Come with me now and explore how God, as a caring parent, worked in my life to bind up my wounds, and consider how he can work in yours.

Why Divorce Is Like a Big Black Hole

When I was six years old I suffered another painful hole, but that time it was in my tooth. My mother suspected a cavity and took me to the dentist. I hated the antiseptic smells, the stark white office, the high-pitched machines, and especially Dr. Worsely. When he came at me with the drill, I squirmed and squealed. Then he slapped me. Subdued and crying, I sat in the chair while he filled my tooth. Even with the Novocain, I felt every bit of the sharp, shooting pain.

Mom consoled me afterward, advising me that if I took good care of my teeth my filling should last thirty or forty years or more. I hoped to be an old lady before I ever had to go to the dentist again, but it was less than four years later when I lost my filling.

I was walking to school and about halfway there, at the crosswalk of our neighborhood's main street, I felt something strange rolling around in my mouth. I pulled out the silver filling. I was shocked! How did that happen? My tongue darted immediately to the spot where it had been and found a large, gaping hole. Shock turned into terror as I realized I'd have to return to the dentist who slapped me.

I stood stuck at the crosswalk, my mind racing. I couldn't go back home because Mom and Dad were at work. I couldn't go to school in this condition. What if my whole tooth fell out? What if all my teeth fell out? Anger mixed with my fear. This wasn't fair! The filling was supposed to last practically forever! Dr. Worsely was supposed to have been a good dentist. I hated him for failing me and making me face pain again.

I started crying. I scanned the sea of cars driving past to see if someone would help me. As I blinked back my tears, I looked at the man in the car right in front of me waiting for the light to turn green. It looked like my dad's car, and the man looked like my dad. It *was* my dad! I screamed as loud as I could, "DA-DD-Y!"

My father heard me, pulled over his car, and scooped me up in his strong arms. Shaking and sobbing I buried my head in his shoulder and clung to him tightly, the silver filling still clutched in my fist. When I finally caught my breath and tearfully told him my tale, he said, "Don't worry, Rosie, everything will be all right. I'm here." I felt calm and safe in his arms.

The Pain of Divorce

My experience with the lost filling reminds me of divorce. When we first married, we were convinced we could trust our husbands. We expected our marriage to last a lifetime, but when it came loose and fell apart, we were frozen with fear, worry, or anger. Sometimes we want to go back, but we can't, yet we can't move ahead either. We may hate our spouses for leaving us, for passively making us leave them, and for the future pain we know we will endure. Our emotions can overtake us, keeping us stuck at the intersection between the hope of dreams and the pain of divorce.

But remember, someone out there will help us. We need to take a deep breath, blink back our tears, and look straight ahead into the face of our Father. Seeing him is not enough though. We must call out to him—scream if we have to—and then submit to his embrace. Real faith is knowing that he will take us into his arms and make it all better.

What If Your Dad Was Not There for You?

Maybe, as a child, you didn't have a loving father on whom you could rely. Your dad was never there for you, or there only part of the time. He may have emotionally, physically, sexually, or verbally abused you. Our image of God is always colored by our relationships with both parents. Our attachment to our mothers began in the womb and may have grown through nursing and nurturing. The bond with our dads, whether healthy or not, was built over time. Similarly we have a natural tie to our Heavenly Father, but we may need to build, or rebuild, our emotional relationship.

Randy Carlson, the popular "Parent Talk" radio talk show host, in his book *Father Memories* advises:

"Fathers leave a lasting impression on the lives of their children. Picture fathers all around the world carving their initials into their family trees. Like a carving in the truck of an oak, as time passes the impressions fathers make on their (daughters) grow deeper and wider. Depending on how the tree grows, those impressions can either be ones of harmony or ones of distortion.

"Some fathers skillfully carve beautiful message of love, support, solid discipline, and acceptance into the personality core of their children. Others use words and actions that cut deeply and leave emotional scars. Time may heal the wound and dull the image, but the impression can never be completely erased. The size, shape, and extent of your father's imprint on your life may be large or small, but it is undeniably there."[1]

Although I had a warm and loving father, he worked long hours to support a wife and eight children. As the oldest, I had to help my mother with the rest of the kids. I often felt that, although Dad loved me, he'd left me alone to take care of myself. My mother was bright, beautiful, and highly educated, but did not connect emotionally with her children. She and I had opposite temperaments, and she could never understand me or meet my emotional needs.

Although I always loved God, I entered adulthood—and my marriages—with the thinking that God loved me but expected me to be a big girl and handle as much as possible by myself. I trusted him to take care of me materially, as my parents did, but not emotionally, as my parents could not. In dating and marriage, I tried on my own to get all my emotional needs met, leading to disaster after disaster, divorce after divorce.

God Cares

Because we're women, because we're human, and because our emotions have been damaged (especially through divorce), we can tend to draw away from men. Many of us loathe to see God as father because of our own fathers' failings, and we even resist seeing God as a man because of the obvious hurt, abandonment, or rejection we have felt. For the past thirty years, women's groups (fueled by genuine and perceived hurts) have caused further harm by nursing a sinful bitterness toward a male-dominated society and a patriarchal church.

Some sisters are more emotionally comfortable with the image of God as mother. From early centuries, a damaged view of men has driven women to worship female deities, the Divine Feminine, and most recently the New Age Goddess within. Women today spend billions of dollars on books, clothing, artifacts, and accessories to connect with the female side of spirituality. They tune in devotedly to Oprah and embrace the not-really-new feminine religion, trying to free themselves through their own inner power. Unfortunately, their genuine desire for a higher power is often laced with the arsenic of female pride and ego.

Both men and women were wired by the Creator to desire him. Most of us acknowledge the One True God, although some of us have difficulty putting a masculine face on him. Yet there is no separate Divine Goddess. There is one God who possesses all the strengths and none of the weaknesses of both powerful manhood and spectacular womanhood. We were all made in his image. When we reject the masculine, we reject God.

This book is intended to help heal emotional wounds so that hurting little girls in grown-up bodies can climb into their Father's lap. God is like a caring parent, with all the loving female and male strengths; he is warm and soft, strong and powerful. He *can* meet all our needs, and he *doesn't* want us to do it alone.

A Father's Love

I've opened each chapter with a "love letter" from your Heavenly Father. His letter, written just for you, is based on his comforting words found in Scripture. He wants to help you through the ups and downs of divorce and of being single again. In my own journey past divorce and into his arms, I have found that he is calling us all to himself, first as *Father,* then as *Healer,* and finally as the ultimate *Lover* of our hearts and souls.

Because we often respond to our life circumstances according to our damaged emotions rather than according to what we know or believe, I've ended each chapter with a reminder to replace our fear with our faith. This always helps bring me back into my Father's arms. I hope it helps you, too.

What Does My Fear Say?

No one will help me through the turmoil. I'm scared, I'm hurting, and I just know it's going to get worse. I feel all alone.

What Does My Faith Say?

My Heavenly Father is always there. He knows exactly what I need and he will help if only I will look up through my tears and call out to him. Whether I whisper or scream, he will hear me, any day, any night, any time at all.

Love Letter

MY LITTLE ONE,

Come close and let me place my hands upon you. I will heal your broken heart and bind up all your wounds. Turn to me today. If you will listen to my voice and do what is right in my eyes, I will bring an end to your pain. For I, the Lord, am your Healer.

Your Loving Father

ᴖ 2 ᴖ

God As Healer

J flew to the Midwest to visit my little brother, Fred, one of the top spine surgeons in the United States. Fred picked me up at the airport and told me he either could drop me off at his home to visit with his wife and their kids, or I could go with him to the Children's Hospital, where he'd just been called in for an emergency procedure. He would outfit me as a medical student and I could watch him perform the surgery. "Are you kidding? Let's go!" I agreed excitedly, without stopping to think about what I was going to see.

Wearing blue scrubs, booties, cap and mask, I stood by Fred alongside a gurney while he talked to the patient, a twelve-year-old boy. The boy's leg had been almost severed just below the knee in a playground accident. Dr. Fred assured him everything would be okay, and he was quickly wheeled into the operating room.

Four days earlier, the emergency room doctors had sewn him up and sent him home. Unexpectedly, the boy had developed a high fever and when it reached 105 degrees the parents, worried and in tears, brought him back. It turned out the improperly cleaned wound was still filled with gravel, and some of the skin around the sutures had died and necrosis was spreading to healthy tissue. The boy's body was racked with infection, and the fever had signaled what was going on behind those stitches.

I'll never forget watching a sight that was together the most gruesome and most awesome I think I'll ever see. Within minutes the medical team had the boy under general anesthesia, draped, and ready for surgery. I was shocked at how aggressively Fred removed the stitches, reopened the wound, and stuck his sterilized and gloved hand right down into the boy's bloody leg to clean it out. As I stood nearby, I watched as my baby brother's skilled fingers quickly cleaned around flesh and bone and then delicately cut away dead tissue that was infecting the rest of the leg. After the wound was cleansed, Fred directed the assistant surgeon to close up while we left to find the boy's parents. The operation went well, Fred told them, and he gave the mom and dad steps for follow-up care at home.

Why Divorce Isn't Always Healed Property

Divorce is like that boy's injury. It's never an intended hurt, but more like a terrible, unexpected accident, usually ripping apart family members and leaving a trail of emotional blood and guts. Too often we are quick to bind up the wounds and move on instead of getting to the deepest levels of pain and allowing God to heal us completely. After all, we've got jobs to do, kids to raise, and bills to pay, and life goes on. We're often ashamed of the fact that we have been divorced, and we tell ourselves, or our loved ones tell us, "Get on with it!" . . . "You'll get over it." . . . "Next year you'll feel better." But that's not usually the case.

Some of us have been carrying the unhealed wounds of divorce for years and the infection has spread, as it always does, into other areas of our lives. That's why it's so important to reach deep into the wound to clean it out properly. If you're a mother, imagine your children as part of your family's healthy tissue. Failure to address the deepest emotional issues of your own divorce undoubtedly will cause the infection to be passed to them, the next generation. They will pick up on your attitudes and get caught in the middle of raging emotions. Even if you don't have children, the hurt, pain, and bitterness of divorce can spread slowly into other healthy relationships.

In his book *Before a Bad Goodbye*, Dr. Tim Clinton, President of the American Association of Christian Counselors, encourages parents considering divorce to examine the devastating effect on their children. "Parents, at times, take such a selfish, cavalier attitude toward the child-casualties of divorce,"[1] says Clinton.

You may not ever think of yourself as a selfish parent, and you may have divorced to protect your children. But it would be selfish to rush yourself through, or even ignore, the healing process just to avoid the pain. Being emotionally disabled and in need of healing makes you less available to meet your children's emotional needs. Your complete emotional healing is something that is necessary to keep your children from being infected with further emotional upheaval and even permanent psychological damage.

One woman I counseled bemoaned how her bitterness toward men hurt her daughters. "My girls are afraid of relationships now. Neither of them trusts men. I never thought that they would pattern their attitudes after my own. I told them many times that they didn't have to experience the pain I did. I encouraged them to find their own loves and I told them that God wanted the best for them. But they were damaged emotionally because I failed to find healing for myself, and I infected them."

Our physical health, too, usually suffers as we experience sleeplessness, headaches, eating problems, and addictions. Work can become even more stressful. Friendships can become damaged and we may start unhealthy new relationships. Even new marriages will be affected by the poison of untreated divorces.

Sue, a divorcée, emailed me, "I wish I had spent more time discovering my emotional problems. I didn't want to admit I had any. I didn't want to be in pain anymore, and I was sick and tired of working on problems of any kind. I just wanted to have fun again. I wasn't really ready to date, and I rushed into marrying Bob. Guess what? Now I feel like I'm back in the same hell with a different man."

All Kinds of Women Are Hurting

Maybe you are a newly divorced mom struggling as a single parent. Perhaps you are single with no children, and your home is empty of love of any kind. You may be older and have been divorced for many years, but deep down inside you're still hurt or bitter. Some of us have been divorced more than once and we're terrified of making another mistake. I know many women who initiated their divorce after years of abuse, and they are so relieved to be away from the turmoil, that they assume they have no unhealed hurts.

Healing of the heart is like physical healing; it happens in layers. Our emotions are at first raw, and some of us move more quickly than others to cover the wound. Florence Littauer's book, *Personality Plus*, helps explain why some women respond differently to their divorce:

"*Popular Sanguine* personalities just want to have fun, keep life on the light side, and charm everyone into loving and adoring them. After a divorce they are quick to forgive and make friends again with their ex and pretend their pain is not as bad as it really is. They will bounce right back and hum "Zippedy do-dah" all day long . . . until anywhere from six months to a few years later, when they find themselves bursting into tears for no reason. They often are afraid to dig deep into their wound and face the process of real healing.

"*Powerful Choleric* personalities, like the Sanguine, tend to be optimistic and quickly move on with the rest of their lives. They thrive on work, accomplishing goals, and they distract themselves with their career, school, child-raising, and a multitude of other projects. They don't waste time being depressed; it's not efficient! No one has to tell them to get on with it because they already have, often too fast and too soon. They almost enjoy the constant fighting with the ex-spouse because they love a challenge and want to win. Because they are quick to anger, through the years they will find themselves years snapping at coworkers and barking orders to the kids, unaware that they rushed too quickly through the healing process.

"The *Perfect Melancholy* personalities, unlike the outgoing Sanguine and Choleric personalities, tend to be introverted. They are often the long-suffering martyr and the most obviously depressed. If they haven't cut emotional ties with the ex, they sometimes harbor secret longings to get back together, and they will outwardly dramatize their very real suffering. Where the Choleric and Sanguine women quickly stuff or cut off their feelings, Melancholys wear their broken hearts on their sleeves. They are not always motivated to heal because they sometimes delight in the misery. After others get tired of hearing about their divorce, they get even more depressed because no one really understands the depth of their suffering.

"The *Peaceful Phlegmatics*, also introverts, just want peace and quiet, and will tend to avoid conflict at any cost. Easygoing and friendly in nature, they are often quick to pretend they are fine after divorce because they don't want to face the hard work of recovery. Phlegmatics can find contentment at almost any level, a strength in some circumstances, but not when deep emotional or spiritual work needs to be done. If healing from divorce requires hard work, they may find ways to accept their brokenness and never take steps to find true healing. You might often hear a passive Phlegmatic woman say, 'Well, this divorce was God's will and there's nothing I can do about it.'"[2]

Do you see yourself in any of these personality capsules? I'm a combination of the Popular Sanguine and Powerful Choleric. After divorce, I struggled to quit pretending life was all rosy and sweet and to accept that I needed more emotional growth and recovery. Thank goodness my Choleric side thrives on challenges, so as soon as I got rid of all the busy distractions, I could get to work on real healing.

Perhaps you've been avoiding complete healing. Maybe you've tried to stitch up your own wounds, and the emotional infection remains. The good news is that you don't have to be a doctor to find healing. Remember, God is the Master Physician. And this book offers practical and spiritual comfort and counsel. God can use it to help stitch you up and send you home with directions, along with prescribed medication such as books, tapes, and counseling for every topic you need.

Don't let that emotional fever continue. Complete healing takes time, but, meanwhile, God's grace helps numb the pain. Take it one day at a time, resting in him while he takes care of the basics. As you read this book, imagine yourself resting comfortably in a warm, cozy hospital bed, in a private room, of course. Your children are cared for, all your bills are paid, and you have some time alone with him. Take a deep breath, let it out slowly, and let the Master Physician begin to heal you *his* way. Are you ready?

What Does My Fear Say?

I can't see any future happiness . . . ever. I doubt this pain will ever end. Nothing will make the hurt or emptiness go away. I'm doomed to feel like this forever.

What Does My Faith Say?

God knows the plans he has for me, a future filled with hope. The pain will end, if I let God help me. Do I believe that?

Love Letter

MY SWEET DAUGHTER,

I know the depth of loss that you have suffered. I know the terrible anguish this failed relationship has caused you and your whole family. It's normal for you to feel deprived and depleted. I created you to desire good things and to ache for what you have lost. Yet, Sweet One, I want your desire to be for me. I want you to ache to have me in your heart, in your life. I am your only sufficiency. I can restore all good things to you and meet all your needs.

Your Loving Father

3

Loss

"It's a wonder Job never committed suicide," I thought sarcastically as I tried to wade through the depressing biblical account of injustice and loss. I was still struggling emotionally and wondering why, after these long months of counseling, prayer, and reading every divorce book I could get my hands on, I was not further along in my recovery. I'd decided that reading the book of Job would comfort and console me, and put my pity into perspective. Instead his story served to bring up even more of my own unhealed emotions. Wallowing in pity, I put down the Bible, got a pen and pad, and started writing a list of losses from my divorce.

My husband had gone into deep depression, struggling over buried childhood issues, for several years before he left. As a result, he'd lost his job and wasn't able to help pay our bills. He left me with all the debt, the house went into foreclosure during the recession, and I had to file bankruptcy. When I moved from my large house to a little apartment with a tin-roof carport, I went into culture shock. My twenty-five year history of good credit went down the tubes, and I couldn't even qualify for a normal car loan. My business also was affected when some of my suppliers cut me off.

Now that I was single, I didn't belong to the same social circles. I had lost friends and relationships, including the couples groups at church. A rumor started that I was having affairs with the married men and even our pastor! Men talked to me differently and women eyed me with suspicion. Despite my wealth of wisdom about love, romance, relationships, marriage, child raising, and stepparenting, I no longer was invited to teach or share my experiences in these areas.

I'd lost the man I had loved, my beautiful home, my financial security and material goods, my car, my credit, my status in the community, my reputation at church, my credibility in the publishing world, and even loving relationships with in-laws.

One of the deepest pains was the loss of my stepson. During our marriage I faced infertility and the fact I never would have children of my own. My husband's son was two years old when I came into his life, and for nearly ten years he had been *my* son, too. After the divorce, I no longer received mother's pins for his Boy Scout badges, Mother's Day presents, or the flowers he used to pick for my birthday. Never again would I be part of his birthday parties, Christmas mornings, school plays, or parent-teacher conferences. I didn't fit into the Mom's group at church anymore, and I even would miss his playmates who often spent the night in our home. I wasn't there on his first day at high school or there to take pictures as he left for his first prom. My dreams for our family died with the divorce. Although my ex-husband recognizes his son's need to still see me, and we enjoy regular visits, I lost my baby in the divorce and still miss him terribly.

Facing Reality

As I wrote down each loss, I felt the anger rise and I wrote faster and more furiously. A funny thing happened, though, as the list grew longer. I was shocked to actually see on paper the many different kinds of losses from divorce. My anger began to fade, and I was overwhelmed with a deep, almost motherly compassion for myself. No wonder I was still struggling emotionally! It was a miracle I wasn't glassy-eyed and in bed slippers, shuffling down the hall of some mental institution listening to soft strains of elevator music on the intercom.

Taking inventory of my losses made me realize that, even though divorce is common, and we have become increasingly desensitized to it, it remains a terrible devastation. My list gave me permission to slow down and allow the healing process to take all the time it needed. I'd been hit harder than I'd thought.

In an excellent workbook entitled *Fresh Start Divorce Recovery Workbook*, Bob Burns and Tom Whiteman describe the devastation of divorce: "You have had a nuclear bomb dropped on your life. It will take awhile for the fallout to settle, but you can survive it if you take the proper steps."[1] Many other counseling experts concur with Burns and Whiteman that divorce is as traumatic as death. Excuse me for disagreeing, but I think it's *worse* than death!

If your spouse dies, you face many losses, but he or she didn't choose to leave you (except in cases of suicide). He didn't slam the door in your face, scream obscenities at you, or quietly live a double life of lies and secrets. Following a death, people come over with casseroles and cookies and the insurance settlement is promptly paid. After divorce, people avoid you and getting regular child support from a living ex-spouse is an ongoing nightmare. A dead husband's ghost doesn't fight with you about who gets the kids on the weekend, and you never have to drop your kids off at the cemetery and see your ex with his new live-in "ghoul-friend!" The problems of divorce go on and on and on, even into the lives of adult children and grandchildren.

Jeannie, a divorced mother and grandmother, shared, "I believe divorce is the hardest loss I have ever gone through, and I have been through all kinds of pain. I lost my two-year-old grandson to cancer, but I know he is with the Lord. Divorce goes on and on. I believe death is easier because there is no continued loss."

Where death is the end, divorce is the beginning of a steady stream of rejection, pain, and loss administered like an ongoing emotional IV drip, poisoning the entire family. And you think you don't need lots of time to heal?

Most therapists agree that reaching emotional stabilization, depending on the individual, takes a minimum of two to three years, and usually about one year for every four to five married. While this is not set in stone, it is a generally reliable guideline, and has proven true in my own divorce recovery and those of the women I counsel.

The following is a list of losses affecting almost every divorced woman. I encourage you to note which ones you have experienced and to add your own.

- *Loss of acceptance.* A spouse's rejection communicates that you are unacceptable, you don't fit in, you don't matter, you are not important, and you have little value. Ever since Adam and Eve were rejected from the garden, we all have been searching for permanent acceptance.
- *Loss of love.* Love is the deepest level of acceptance. With divorce it seems that the whole world knows that your spouse does not love you. The movies, magazines, and media all tell you that you need love, but no one loves you. It often doesn't matter that family and friends love you; the love of your life is gone.
- *Loss of self-esteem.* If you have no doubts about who you are in Christ and what you did to try to make your marriage work, loss of self-esteem may be minimal. For some, though, the shame, guilt, and regret eats away at you. When a man leaves you, either emotionally or physically, it's common for you to *feel* as if you are not attractive, lovable, and desirable . . . even if you *know* you are.
- *Loss of a sense of belonging.* You and your husband created and were part of a whole family unit, and now you're not. If you have no children, you have lost that family completely. Many of you with children get so absorbed in your immediate family that you might fail to maintain other strong family ties. Divorce can leave you feeling totally disconnected.
- *Loss of your husband.* Your husband became "one flesh" with you. A husband is intended to be part of his wife, spiritually,

emotionally, sexually, and physically. Now that part of you is gone and you have no control over it.

- *Loss of your lover.* You no longer have a lover to hold you, love you, caress you, or play with and tease you. No one to satisfy you emotionally, physically, or sexually. Another's touch will not be the same—no substitute can compare. Frustration mixes with anger, hurt, and deep longing.

- *Loss of someone to love.* Loving someone is as important as having someone love *you*. For mothers, it is a little easier to transfer to your children that time, attention, and energy that used to go to your man. Women without children may experience an even deeper need for someone—*anyone*—to love.

- *Loss of your provider.* Even if you were the major breadwinner, your husband probably contributed to your lifestyle financially and took care of many of your household needs, such as opening jars of pickles and lifting heavy boxes. Now he's gone. Your helper, your caretaker, has slammed the door in your face either by his leaving, his selfishness, or his apathy. Maybe you shut the door yourself, leaving for reasons that seemed right. Either way, you're on your own.

- *Loss of your protector and partner.* Did you appreciate having a man's physical and emotional protection? Now when you buy a used car, you no longer have his help and men say and do things that they would not when your husband was with you. Maybe he did things around the house that you cannot, so now you must hire outside help. Even if you feel self-assured in these areas, don't you miss having a partner?

- *Loss of companionship.* Sitting in front of the TV in the evenings or reading together was so comfortable. Now you laugh alone at the movie, and have no one with whom to share newspaper headlines in the mornings. You probably don't bother to cook something special for yourself, and it's easier to just throw some hot dogs in the pot for the kids.

- *Loss of your children.* Some women lose custody of their children. Others lose chunks of time through the visitation schedules.

Having your children at home each day and night can give you companionship and control over their safety, while sending them away on weekends to be with people you don't know can be unsettling. Even stepmoms' hearts can be ripped out when they lose children through divorce.

- *Loss of the hope for future children.* Did you dream of having more children? The loss of a marriage also can be the loss of children you had hoped for. Give yourself permission to count the loss of these real people, too.
- *Loss of your children's loyalty.* In an intact family, children usually don't take sides, assess their parent's marriage, or judge their actions. With divorce, the marriage often is publicly aired for the whole family, and children often voluntarily choose, or are forced to choose, to take sides. They might "betray" you by acting as a spy for the other parent, or in other ways.
- *Loss of control over your children.* They go to his house on weekends now and you have no control over what they see, hear, or do. It's scary. What does he tell them about you? Who will protect them?
- *Loss of financial security.* Income is halved, pensions are split, and retirement funds are drained for attorney's fees. Sometimes you fear you never will recover financially and are doomed to poverty for life.
- *Loss of lifestyle.* You were used to private schools for the children, vacations at the beach, and dinner out every weekend. Now you can barely afford school backpacks. You may feel like crying because you can't get your nails done anymore. Don't let anyone tell you that it's a small thing—you have a right to *feel* like it's a big thing.
- *Loss of time.* Perhaps you didn't have a job when you were married, and now you are thrown into the workplace. Or you worked, but now you come home and handle everything by yourself. You don't have the time for the rest, fun, friends, prayer, reading, and recreation necessary for a balanced life.

- *Loss of home.* Do you miss your big kitchen and dining room and the lovely yard? Maybe you finally had painted your house exactly the way you wanted, installed the new dishwasher, or planted rose bushes, but now you live elsewhere. Whether big or small, every loss is real.
- *Loss of good credit.* If you are self-employed, like me, divorce might have affected your business credit and your ability to smoothly handle cash flow. Loss of financial stability seems like loss of power over your own life.
- *Loss of friends and relatives.* Can you maintain friendships with his former friends and his family? Even if many of his friends and family remain gracious, your social life may have drastically changed. Have other relationships ended because of the divorce?
- *Loss of family approval and acceptance.* Maybe your parents really liked your ex-husband or are angry that you have put the kids through this. Maybe they have quit talking to you. Many women suffer the loss of close family support and find themselves not only wounded by the divorce, but under attack by relatives.
- *Loss of role in the community.* As Mrs. So-and-So, you may have had privileges at his workplace, stores, clubs, and in other social settings. You may also now be prohibited from volunteer or other community work that you enjoyed. Are you excluded from any social events now?
- *Loss of role in the church.* Did you belong to a couples or married group at church? Count the loss of those times and friendships. Some churches will ask you to step down from a ministry which you hold dear and for which God has equipped you. Tremendous loss can accompany that form of rejection.
- *Loss of reputation.* Do you get looks or whispers? Have rumors been spread about you on social circles? Have you been shunned at church, at school, in the ladies lunch group or other places in the community? A loss of reputation hurts.

- *Loss of social status.* Even if your credit is still good, as a single or divorced woman you might have to pay higher insurance rates, fall in different risk categories, and be assumed "less stable" than married people. That's a definite loss!

- *Loss of credibility.* Were you regarded as having wisdom about marriage, communication, commitment, or other areas? Did you mentor young couples, teach, write, speak, or counsel others about marriage? Have you experienced a loss of believability by outsiders?

- *Loss of dreams and goals.* Did you plan for a cabin on the lake, college for your kids, or a mid-life career? Maybe you were simply hoping to send the kids to camp for their very first time. You might have to kiss those dreams good-bye, too. If you're older and near retirement, you might not look forward to driving that RV around the country by yourself. As selfish as that might sound to someone who can't even afford a vacation, loss of future hopes and dreams is as real for the rich as for the poor.

- *Loss of hope for another marriage.* Younger women tend to assume there is still plenty of time to find another mate. Older women aren't so sure and sometimes feel desperation and despair. Where do you fit in?

- *Loss of sleep.* A major contributor to depression after divorce is the inability to sleep through the night without tossing, turning, crying, or feeling angry. Armies have used sleep deprivation as a form of torture. This loss can compound all your other losses.

- *Loss of health.* In divorce, the only loss you might enjoy is a few extra pounds. But rapid or steady weight loss from not eating is not healthy. Neither is weight gain, headaches, skin problems, irritable bowels, muscle aches, loss of energy, unclear thinking, or an inability to concentrate. These and other common health losses can further intensify your grief in a divorce.

- *Loss of emotional security in spiritual matters.* God always loves us and will never leave us. But with divorce, no matter how good you were or how hard you tried, you might feel that God is disappointed with you, critical of who you are, and punishing you for your failed marriage.

Can you see now that in divorce you have taken a huge hit, mentally, emotionally, physically, sexually, financially, and spiritually? Don't let anyone tell you to hurry up and move on, to get over it, to get a life. Don't let them tell you everything is not as bad as it seems and everything will be okay. It *is* bad and it never will be the same. There. You said it. It's not selfish or self-absorbed to take a good hard look at the damages you have sustained. Every doctor does exactly that with the patients in the trauma ward of a hospital and the diagnosis is not minimized. Before surgery, therapy, or healing can occur, the x-ray *must* be taken.

Taking Your Own Emotional X-Ray

Now is a good time to make your own list of losses. Review this chapter and see if you can identify with or add to the list. You can complete this exercise with your children as well, teaching them how to face and accept their losses. I also encourage you to share with them the Faith and Fear applications at the end of each chapter.

When you are ready (which you may not be until you get through other chapters in this book or are further along in your healing process), give the list to your Heavenly Father. He already knows your losses, but he wants you to give him that list anyway. He wants you to trust that he not only will restore what you have lost, but he will give you even greater blessings. You don't really believe that right now? That's okay. For now, keep believing it in your head. Eventually your feelings will follow.

What Does My Fear Say?

I have lost everything I ever held dear. I have lost everything that I need, that any woman needs. I will never, ever get it back, and I am doomed to a miserable life because of my divorce.

What Does My Faith Say?

In losing these things, God is asking me to draw nearer to him. Sometimes those things actually prevented my being closer to him. Stripped of all I hold dear, he can clothe me in his pure love and prepare me for even greater gifts! All I need to do is trust and wait, even though I don't feel like it right now . . . and that's okay.

Love Letter

DAUGHTER,

I know sometimes you are scared to face reality. You fear letting go of what you wanted for so long. You are holding tightly to what you want, not necessarily what I want for you.

Come here and sit by me, and let me hold your hand. Do you feel my power? I can break that hard fear . . . if you will let me.

Your Loving Father

4

Shock and Denial

When Joyce walked into the DivorceCare meeting, I could see pain written all over her face. Any group has talkers and watchers, and Joyce was definitely a talker. True to her Choleric personality, she usually had good insight into the other group members' problems and frequently offered down-to-earth advice. Although she was blunt, she had a gift for getting to the bottom line, which sometimes helped shock the others into facing and dealing with the reality of their individual situations. But one thing was wrong with Joyce: she remained in shock and denial about her *own* divorce.

As the weeks went by, we noticed that Joyce rarely revealed anything about her situation. Phyllis, another Choleric personality, decided she'd had enough of Joyce's advice to the others and blurted out one night, "Well, Joyce, what's your story?" The room grew quiet and all eyes were on Joyce as she finally told us about her pain.

Joyce was in her fifties and had been married for more than thirty years, with two grown children and an ex-husband who was living with another woman. Joyce broke down and cried as she told how her husband had brought his girlfriend to their son's wedding, something no divorced woman wants to endure. Although Joyce had told us their divorce had happened only a few months ago, we found out that her husband had moved out several years ago and was engaged to this new woman. It became apparent that Joyce had begun to face the reality of the divorce only when the legal paperwork had become final just a few months prior. As clear-headed as she was regarding others' situations, Joyce was stuck in denial about her own.

The Grieving Process

Elisabeth Kubler-Ross first popularized the stages of grief in her book *On Death and Dying*. Although others have expanded formulas for charting what happens to us after a crisis event such as an accident, disease, death, or divorce, Kubler-Ross simplified the stages into *Denial* (shock), *Anger, Bargaining, Depression,* and finally *Acceptance*. [1] We usually fall back and forth between these stages in our journey through grieving and recovery, but the very first step is always shock and denial. No one can come to a place of healing until they pass through this dream-like stage. Because our wills are so strong and powerful, we can stay stuck in denial (whether we realize it or not) for years, refusing to face reality and creating an alternate world of reality. Joyce was a classic example.

The Wedding Ring

Once the floodgate of Joyce's emotions was opened, she began to share more and more of her pain, anger, and confusion in our weekly meetings. Soon the other group members tired of her complaints and wanted her to move on but I asked them to be patient with her. At DivorceCare meetings, we watch a thirty-minute video before our group support and discussion, and one night I announced that next week's video was on new relationships. Joyce remarked that she was nowhere near ready for that. We all encouraged her to return, though, and watch the video, and she did.

When the lights came on after the video and people started for their cookies and coffee, Joyce sat glumly at the table, with deep furrowed pain on her face, absent-mindedly fingering her wedding ring. No one else had ever come to our group still wearing a ring. I asked how she felt about the video, and she mumbled a sarcastic remark. Then I told her I noticed she still wore her wedding ring and asked if she'd thought about taking it off. Suddenly she burst into tears, her shoulder sagged, and her face fell into her hands as she sobbed uncontrollably, holding tight to her ring finger. The group sat shocked and silent as I immediately got up, stood behind her and put my arms around her. "Shhhh-shhhh" I whispered as a mother to her child, patting her gently. After a few minutes I came back around, sat down, held both her hands in mine, looked her right in the eyes, and said, "Joyce . . ." I paused, letting her catch her breath and stop crying, "I want you to think about going home tonight and taking off your ring." She looked up, wide-eyed and still teary, in absolute horror at the thought.

"You don't have to take it off for good—just practice," I said. "When you are on your bed tonight, take off the ring and leave it on the bed stand for two minutes. Then you can put it back on. If that's really difficult, imagine Jesus sitting right next to you with his hand around your shoulder, lovingly watching you slip it off. Every night, try to leave it off a little longer. That's all. Give yourself permission to go as slow as you want. Just do a little every night, okay?"

She nodded silently.

I wondered all week how Joyce was doing with her scary assignment, but I knew she needed something to shock her out of her state of denial. Before she arrived at the next meeting, some of the group members started talking about Joyce, wondering how she was and if she would ever come back to our group. Well, we were all in for a big surprise! Joyce fairly waltzed in with a big smile on her face and a plate of fresh-baked brownies. We all glanced at her hand and noticed the ring was gone! Joyce was a new woman. Phyllis came up to her at the break and said, "Joyce, you look beautiful! When you first started coming here there was so much pain in your eyes. Tonight, I have to tell you, you look like a different person." Joyce smiled, cocked her head a little, looked around at everyone else who was smiling back, and grinned from ear to ear.

*J*t Hurts to Hold On

Take your hand right now and make a fist. Tighter! Dig those nails into your palm and hold it as long as you can. Keep holding! Now let go, and feel the instant relief. Denial is like clinging hard and fast to a reality that we have lost, and we only hurt ourselves in the long run. Remember, with a closed, tight fist we can't hold anyone's hand, and God can't fill it with surprises.

Connie admits that she stayed stuck in denial because she didn't want to face the alternative. "He was cheating on me for at least the second time. I had thought we were getting along well. We were involved in church, etc. I later found out he was seeing my best friend."

Can our husbands really be seeing our best friends and we don't have a clue? Yes, if we focus on the exterior behaviors like church attendance and "getting along well" to help us stay in denial. Sometimes there isn't a clue, but more often than not, women later admit that there were signs all over the place. One woman told me she was in denial most of her marriage because they never fought.

Denial can feel safe, but it's not. Inevitably, with the passing of time, things get worse. Most women who admit to having been in denial in some area wish that they'd faced the pain when it was still small. Did you know that denial is rooted in fear and pride? "I'm scared to face reality . . . and I refuse to trust God to help me make it through."

Joyce is still middle-aged and has more than a few wrinkles, but a beauty has begun to shine through, a beauty that was intended for us all. Joyce still has a way to go in unclenching her fist of denial, but relief was immediate even in the first little step of letting go. Although healing from divorce is largely a mental, emotional, and spiritual process, sometimes a physical act of letting go helps us on our way.

Are you still in shock or denial? Is something holding you back from taking the next step in becoming a whole beauty? You might want to ask God, and even your friends or family who may have an idea or two, to reveal something that will help you especially right now.

What Does My Fear Say?

This can't be real. It isn't happening. I don't believe it. I'm afraid to believe it. I don't want to believe it!

What Does My Faith Say?

My denial about any area of my divorce is secondary to my denial about God's love for me and his promises to heal my heart, no matter how bad it ever gets. I need to learn how to let go and start to trust him.

Love Letter

SWEETHEART,

Dry your tears. Let go of your hurt and anger. Your husband rejected you in many ways, and so have friends, family, and society. Throughout life, people will reject you, in one way or another, because they are imperfect. Most of the time they are hurt and angry, too. For the moment, forget about everyone else and forget the times you have rejected me in the past. Come to me now. Rest your head on my shoulder and feel my arms around you. Know that I love you deeply and passionately, and when you come to me, I never will reject you. Never.

Your Loving Father

❦ 5 ❦

The Rejection Connection

My ex-husband, Tom, wasn't the first man to reject me. When I was five years old and living in a Sacramento suburb, my next-door neighbor Terry, a spunky, freckle-faced, blonde boy, called to me through our wooden fence to come look through the knothole, where he'd show me a surprise. When I ran over and looked through the hole, he stabbed me with a sharp pencil and almost poked my eye out!

I can't remember the physical pain and I have no scar under my right eye. But I had to face the reality that someone who always had been nice and friendly could turn on me in a minute and hurt me badly. Terry was my friend. I just couldn't believe it. I didn't *want* to believe it. Sound familiar?

In a divorce we tend to stay in denial, that first stage of the grieving process, because we desperately want to avoid the pain of rejection. Rejection is older than Adam and Eve; Lucifer first rejected God's authority. Then the first human couple rejected God and suffered from his rejection of their actions. After being separated from God, Adam and Eve and their family spent the rest of their lives making sacrifices and trying to regain acceptance from their Heavenly Father. They longed to feel loved and accepted again, the most precious thing they'd lost in their "divorce" from God. Fortunately, God immediately offered hope of reconciliation through the coming Savior.

If Adam and Eve were like today's couples, they'd also reject each other in many ways and then try to kiss and make up. We've all been caught up in that same cycle ever since.

Why Rejection Is So Painful

Can you imagine the deep pain and shock Adam and Eve must have felt when they, who used to stroll contentedly through the garden with God, found themselves locked out forever and on their own? Rejection hurts because God created us to be in relationship with him and others. In a relationship with him, we find safety, warmth, love, acceptance, joy, and every other good thing.

Since God wired us to be connected to him, mankind will continually search for something or someone, bigger or better, than himself or herself. When we are not connected with God and others, we die physically, emotionally, and spiritually. As God said, "It is not good for the man to be alone" (Gen. 2:18). Marriage, a woman's deepest connection with a man, represents (a pale imitation as it is) the marriage relationship between God and his people, Christ and his bride. Our longing for others is rooted in our longing for him.

Unfortunately, we try to find that perfect and lasting contentment of a relationship with God in human relationships. Women frequently stay in miserable marriages because they fear being alone. They will bend, change, work, pray, and even allow themselves to be abused just so they can avoid the pain of rejection, and yet they are being grossly rejected in many ways.

After divorce the most common mistake we make is filling up that gaping relationship hole with our children or a new romance, or both. Ultimately, all of those human relationships will fail us. No one ever will accept us, love us, put us first, or provide for us the way our Heavenly Father can.

*H*ow Husbands Reject Their Wives

Passive rejection is what a woman with a passive spouse usually experiences: the silent treatment, clamming up, not following through, avoidance, and procrastination. He says he will do something but never does. He writes out checks that bounce and makes promises he doesn't intend to keep. He hates change and avoids conflict.

If your ex-husband put little effort into the marriage, didn't open up, refused to go to counseling, didn't read the books you brought home, waited for you to bring up problems, just couldn't find time to spend with you at that marriage retreat, or thought you two could straighten out your own troubles, then he *passively rejected* you and the marriage. Maybe he brought home a good paycheck, didn't beat you, didn't drink or do drugs, and had no girlfriend on the side, but he isolated himself in the garage or the den most of the time and left you as the head of the family in many ways.

You may have walked out on him, fed up and angry, and filed for divorce. But the real divorce begins when one or both of the partners fails to take whatever steps are needed to build a strong marriage.

Active rejection is more obvious: yelling, screaming, hitting, arguing, cheating, driving away, slamming the door, refusing to move, shaming, and criticizing. Outward instead of inward, these forms of rejection sometimes seem worse, but the effects of either type of rejection can be just as painful and just as damaging. *Both types of behavior are controlling;* one is just less obvious.

If your husband had an affair, frequently threatened you with divorce, stayed out with the guys most of the time, pursued his own interests, put the children, his parents, or friends ahead of you in almost all circumstances, and controlled all the money, he *actively rejected* you and the marriage.

Some husbands reject their wives passively and actively.

To the outside world, and sometimes even in our DivorceCare meetings, an unspoken stigma is attached to the dumpee, the person who physically left the home and filed for divorce. It's often unfairly assumed that the person who left or filed carries more blame than the other does. Each of us needs to take a good look at our own situation and realize that we probably rejected each other for a long time, not fully understanding why or how we were doing it.

When I asked women what types of rejection they had experienced during and after their divorce, from their ex, the kids, or anyone else, I noticed they fell into two categories. Perhaps you can relate to most or even all of these:

Passive Rejection

My ex doesn't call when he's late bringing the kids back home. —*Mary*

The child support payment is always late and never the right amount. —*Sue*

I was left off the guest list for the Ladies Lunch Bunch because everyone else is married. —*Barbara*

Paul won't even talk to me anymore. He won't return my calls or letters. —*Sarah*

He consistently forgets to send home all the kids' clothes. —*Mona*

He brings his new girlfriend right up to the door every time. —*Cheryl*

He kept the best set of the kids' school photos for himself! —*Marlene*

Active Rejection

My son wants to go live with his father! —*Nina*

Armando ends up screaming at me every time we talk about the kids. —*Sophia*

He tells blatant lies about me to the kids. —*Celeste*

The judge didn't believe me and cut off my alimony and lowered the child support. —*Janie*

My brother and his wife have sided with my ex-husband. —*Janet*

Darryl and his new wife are trying to get full custody! —*Cathy*

He came in the house, snooped around, and took my tools! —*Donna*

When you no longer get the same courtesy, consideration, and communication from your spouse, family, friends, and society in general as you did before the divorce, you are experiencing daily doses of rejection.

In divorce the rejection never ends, and smart women will learn to expect it. Teenagers will want to go live with their father. New stepparents will join the battle against you. He'll remarry someone rich, and they will take that vacation you always dreamed of or buy the house that was supposed to be yours. When the kids get married, you might face rejection at the wedding, and your ex-husband and his new wife will be the first to baby-sit your grandkids!

I remember learning about rejection and realizing that's what my stepson's mother often experienced. She felt rejection every time my stepson came home to her house on Sunday nights and reported what a good time he'd had with Daddy and Rose.

Sometimes he'd go home with a book or toy I'd bought him, and she felt left out. After divorce, it was my turn. On one of my visits with my stepson, he talked about his dad's new girlfriend who had given him a $400 boogie board. There it was again, the same old pattern. Thank goodness I didn't take it personally, or I could have gotten sucked into the rejection connection.

The Rejection Connection

We have a choice. We can either prepare ourselves to handle future rejection or we can continue to let it suck the life out of us. In his book *Rejection Junkies*, Dr. Gary Lawrence, a Christian author, speaker, and radio talk-show host in Phoenix, Arizona, describes the people who reject us as "emotional energy thieves." I liked that word picture so much that I wrote a description of how I felt about the emotional energy thieves in my life, and Gary used it in his book.

"Picture yourself strapped in a chair. As you look down you can see and feel hundreds of long, black electrical cords plugged into your arms, legs, your body, and into the sides and top of your head. You can almost hear the low, pulsating sound of those cords as they suck the strength and energy out of your body. You feel weak, tired, and trapped. Twisting and squirming, you try to break free. You want to scream and rip those cords out, but you can't. Hopeless, you begin to cry." [1]

We can't isolate ourselves from rejection unless we live on a deserted island, so what can we do? We can learn to expect rejection and to insulate ourselves from it. If we don't, two things will happen:

- We will become bitter, hurt, wounded, anxious, angry, depressed, or vengeful, and,
- We will stay emotionally connected through our unresolved bitterness. I like what they teach in Al-Anon and other 12-

step groups: "Don't invite that person to live in your head rent-free!"

Some of us will keep those invisible emotional cords connected by trying to control the other. We'll sic our attorney on our ex to control him in court, or we'll be extra sweet to try to get him to see things our way. Both are forms of manipulation in an effort to avoid his further rejection. We can even be in emotional bondage to our kids out of fear that they'll reject us. Sometimes we try to gain their favoritism or loyalty, such as buying them the new toy we can't really afford, or giving them permission to do something Dad said no to, so they will like us better.

Even without any personal contact, some of us will stay connected through a long-held wounded spirit, anger, or feeling of victimization. We may think we're disconnected because we don't see, hear, or talk to the other person, but the lingering negative emotions keep us plugged in, draining us of a full share of joy. We are still trapped in the *Rejection Connection*.

Dr. Lawrence teaches that the best way to unplug is to realize and focus on your loving, secure relationship with God and to release the other person through forgiveness. Taking that step opened the door for my healing in all past, and even future, relationships. I felt almost giddy the day I sat in Dr. Lawrence's office and clearly saw that I had made other people my god but could now unplug from them and instead tap directly into God's love. I finally had a practical technique for handling my feelings of rejection. I felt free!

Before our divorce, I remember sitting with my husband as we called friends and family members who had hurt us in the past. Not only did we forgive them, but we sought forgiveness from them for our bitter attitudes. This may sound uncomfortable, and you may not want to even think about forgiving people who have rejected (and keep rejecting) you. That's okay. In Chapter 18 we'll talk about the two kinds of forgiveness necessary for full emotional healing.

*W*hat Does My Fear Say?

I can't keep letting people reject me. It hurts too much. I've got to keep trying to get them to like me, accept me, agree with me, and love me. If they don't, I have to find a way to manipulate or control them so I can get what I need and deserve. It's only fair. Oh, but it's so exhausting. I'm so tired of all this.

*W*hat Does My Faith Say?

I have all the strength and power I need when I remember how much God loves me and that he is here to meet all my needs. I can choose to feel safe and insulated from what others say or do to me. I can go to him through prayer and his Word, seeking his counsel, his wisdom. I can choose to unplug from others and plug into the ultimate source of love.

Love Letter

MY CHILD,

I know you are angry. You and your family have suffered so many injustices, and it hurts to think you may face more in the future. Sometimes, you are even angry with me. That's okay, I understand and I have everything in control. I will make all things right in my own time. Will you trust me?

I want you to learn ways to process your anger so that the sun does not go down each day with bitterness still in your heart. If you will listen to me, I will teach you new ways to become slow to speak out harshly and slow to anger. Remember I love you; I will meet your needs; I will teach you through all this.

Your Loving Father

6

Anger

Lori wrote me about the anger she felt when she discovered her husband, a youth pastor, had been arrested for sexually molesting boys in their church. He didn't want counseling, and he didn't want to stay married. Lori realized they had been living a lie for quite a while, and that the real divorce had started a long time ago. The arrest was just the last straw in an ongoing series of rejection.

"The night he was arrested his parents paid his bail. When he came home, I got a chance to talk to him alone and I asked him if he did it. I was irate. I have one heck of a temper at times. I pounded the pillow with my clenched fists as hard as I could and screamed at him at the top of my lungs. I don't even remember what I said. I could tell I scared him, though, because he had never seen such anger. I just wanted to knock the crap out of him. He knew how betrayed and angry I was. We had just bought a house six months earlier, hoping that would help our marriage, and now we had to sell it back to the contractor.

"My husband moved out but came back one day to help me pack everything. The anger that had built up came out again and, after yelling and crying, I told him I had to do one more thing. He asked me not to slap him, so I pounded his back with my fist as hard as I could, over and over and over. Finally he said that was enough, so I stopped. I was shaking and crying and, oh God help me, I wanted to hit him again, but I thought maybe he would press charges against me for physical abuse. I hate to admit it felt good. I felt much better after that, but I was sick to my stomach, too. It wasn't right. The whole thing just wasn't right."

Lori said she'd never before felt or expressed her anger so violently, nor has she since. But she's not the only one who has felt that way. Here is what other women, all with Judeo-Christian beliefs and desires to be good, shared with me:

"In my divorce, the single most difficult emotion for me to handle was anger. My husband had an affair. I was extremely angry with him and his girlfriend, who is now his wife. He ignored our children for a long time after he left us, and now, although he has a relationship with them, his wife is mean to them. I'm angry at her for the way she treats them, and I'm angry at him because he lets it happen." —*Rene*

"My first divorce made me angry because he had an affair and had lied so much about everything. I wanted it to work out. I was angry with myself for not seeing it and for looking like a fool to my friends. In a way, I was relieved when my second marriage ended, but I have not gotten over his abuse and control of the kids and me. I still have a lot of hate for him and a lot of guilt about the things I did. I still flinch when someone near me raises a hand too quickly. Then I get angry at myself!" —*Kim*

Anger —The Other Side of Love

The huge losses in divorce and the ongoing rejection provide plenty to be angry about. There are whole books written on the topic of anger, and one of my favorite is *The Other Side of Love* by Dr. Gary Chapman, who hosts the nationally syndicated radio broadcast, "A Growing Marriage". Dr. Chapman asserts that "anger is not a sin, but flows from God's love—it is his response to injustice." [1] He explains that our anger is evidence that we are made in God's image, and we should thank God for our capacity to experience it.

When my husband left me, he announced he was going away for a few days and said he'd be back later to get his things. I was in shock for only a day, crying for hours on end, and then the anger came. The next morning I called my best friend, Ronda, and said between sobs, "Get over here with some boxes right now!" Ronda spent the morning with me as I went through every room in the house and packed my husband's stuff into brown cardboard cartons. With every drawer, every closet, every memory, I would burst into tears. Then I yelled, cried, and cussed in anger. I remember how I drifted back and forth between wanting to smash his sports memorabilia and then, an instant later, wanting to wrap each piece tenderly so it wouldn't break because I loved him so much.

My anger made me feel good and bad at the same time. I needed to get angry, but I didn't want to stay angry. I realized that anger had both positive and negative attributes. Scripture tells us not to let the sun go down on our anger. I've learned that means that anger is a part of life, but the key is not to carry it over to the next day. How can we do that? First we need to understand exactly what it is. Let's take a look at some aspects of anger:

- Anger is an automatic response, a normal human emotion intended to spur us to constructive action.
- The world thinks anger is an animal instinct that prepares us to deal with danger (fight or flight response), but it's much more than that.
- Anger is part of God's nature.
- Throughout history God has been angry with his people, and his anger always has been rooted in his desire for righteousness and justice.
- Because we're made in his image, our anger also stems from our sense of righteousness and justice.
- Anger is our reaction to injustice, whether it's real or perceived.

- Anger isn't always wrong, it's how we respond to our anger than can be wrong.
- Because of our human nature, our anger can become sin.

Our anger can be a sin when we nurse it into bitterness, and/or we try to define "injustice" in self-centered terms. Here's an example:

Bitterness . . . Jackie is angry that her husband had an affair. Her initial anger is a normal, healthy response to a real injustice. But when Jackie fails, over time, to move toward forgiving her husband and instead tells the world about his faults, her anger becomes a form of bitterness, and bitterness is a sin. Sometimes we hold on to our anger because it allows us to vent other pent-up feelings. If we're not used to releasing anger in healthy ways, we indulge it when it finally comes out, because (like Lori said) it feels good. Sometimes we use anger to help us set or enforce boundaries that we otherwise are too afraid to set.

Defining Justice . . . Jackie is also angry that she no longer can shop at Nordstrom's because her financial status changed after the divorce. It's just not fair! Okay, that's obviously a poor definition of injustice, but many women convince themselves that they deserve the exact same lifestyle they enjoyed before the divorce. They forget that even in good marriages, nothing is guaranteed. Everything we have—even our life's breath—is a privilege, not a right.

Yet we commonly cry injustice when our children can no longer attend their excellent private schools, or they have to quit piano lessons. Unfortunately, even the basics of food, clothing, and a home can become difficult to provide. Sometimes we use such circumstances as an excuse to stay angry with our ex-husbands, the world, or even God. Again, it's not a true injustice that we lose some comforts and privileges. Besides, no matter how noble and pure our needs and wants, we often are only angry because we didn't get our way.

$\mathcal{O}$ld Anger and New Anger

During one weekly DivorceCare session, we watch a video on anger. Through the taped discussion with counseling experts, we learn that we can think we've worked through the anger, gone through the grieving process, and forgiven him . . . but find ourselves still angry. After the video, Elaine shared a revelation about her own situation:

"Five years ago I had forgiven my ex-husband for the divorce and thought I'd processed my anger. Lately, I have been confused to find myself still angry with him, and that's why I came to this class. I realize now that this anger I feel today is separate from what happened back then. I'm angry today because he refuses to honor the boundaries I try to set with him. He shows up late with the kids, doesn't send his check on time, and doesn't call when he says he will. I feel much better knowing I did get over the old anger. I just need to know how to get rid of the new anger."

Elaine's story is common among divorced women. Unless we've been in some kind of ongoing counseling, therapy, or educational process, most of us haven't developed the best communication skills, and we may know almost nothing about how to set and enforce boundaries with anyone, especially our ex-husbands. Instead of learning how to set up a strong, protective wall around ourselves, we use anger like a pit bull to rip apart anyone who steps over the line.

$\mathcal{I}$s Society Boiling Over with Anger?

Is the totality of society enraged today—air rage, road rage, employee rage, surf rage, and even pedestrian rage? Every week we read such headlines as, "Dog Thrown into Traffic by Angry Driver," "Enraged Airline Passenger Causes Flight Mayhem," and "Single Father of Four Pummeled to Death at Youth Hockey Game." Experts who once thought the answer was anger management, now admit that this buzzword only deals with the symptom of deeper problems. Red-hot anger results from self-centered, fearful, and faithless attitudes toward life, coupled with a habit of self-indulgence.

Leon James, professor of psychology at the University of Hawaii and author of *Road Rage and Aggressive Driving* calls our increased tendency toward rage a "culture tantrum," and I couldn't agree more. Swinging to the other end of the parenting pendulum in the last thirty years, we've allowed our children to pitch a fit whenever things don't go their way, afraid to squash their self-esteem. We have failed to teach them to view life realistically and to trust God to meet their needs.

Two Reasons We Still Get Angry

Part of the healing of the heartbreak of divorce is learning how to make sure we don't set ourselves up for or leave ourselves open to new wounds and new anger. We can find ourselves always responding in anger for two reasons:

First, we don't know how to set and enforce healthy boundaries. Drs. Henry Cloud and John Townsend have produced an excellent series of books and cassette tapes titled *Boundaries*, and in Chapter 26 we'll discuss ways to set boundaries after divorce.

Secondly, we hold onto *unrealistic expectations* (mythical thinking). We may find ourselves on a spin-cycle of anger because we continue to hold expectations of other people and life in general that are not consistent with reality. We need to examine our belief system and start making changes, such as:

Unrealistic Expectation #1: My ex-husband *should* pay his child support on time and in full. He knows it makes me angry, and he's doing it to control me!

Change to—My ex never has been on time for anything, and I need to accept that fact without bitterness. If I really trust that God will see me through, I can learn to make my budget work without relying on his prompt payments. I'll see what I can do through the courts (take action), and if it's not much, then I'll let go (release). I can choose to free myself from that control I give him.

Unrealistic Expectation #2: My ex-husband brings his girlfriend to the kids' baseball games. I've told him I do *not* want to sit by her! He's trying to make me mad on purpose.

   Change to—Like all human beings, my ex is going to do what makes him comfortable. If I don't want to sit by his girlfriend, I will sit on the other side, or move down a few seats (take action), without being rude or snotty (release).

Unrealistic Expectation #3: I have asked my ex-husband and his new wife to please send all of the children's clothes and belongings home when they return on Sunday. They just ignore me. I've lost more of the kid's clothes that way and it costs me money!

   Change to—I have no power to make them return the clothes. I'll quit asking and instead work on helping the older children take more responsibility for their things. I won't send over anything I don't mind not seeing again (take action), and then I just won't focus on it anymore (release).

I encourage you to make a list of the things your ex-husband does that anger you and look for "unrealistic expectations" and a "lack of healthy boundaries" on your part. It is good to apply this exercise to anyone with whom you continually find yourself angry: the kids, your mother, and your boss.

*A*ctive or Passive? Even Anger Has Personality

Two women can be equally angry, but one looks it, the other does not. The outgoing personalities usually let us know when they are upset; passive personalities do not. Because anger often is considered a male attribute, some of us don't believe we are feminine if we are angry. As God-fearing members of society, we also don't want to appear angry because *others* might judge us as not being very moral characters. Baloney! I don't advocate indulging our emotions and letting it all hang out in rages, attacks, or even smooth, snide shaming, but I also know how unhealthy it is to stuff and hide our anger. Both extremes can damage us mentally, emotionally, spiritually, and physically (ulcers, headaches, depression, and other maladies). It's not good for us to rant and rave, nor is it healthy to pretend we are not angry, saying "Oh, I'm not angry, I'm just *sad*" or "I'm not angry, I'm just very *disappointed*." The longer we deny our anger, the longer it will take us to heal from divorce.

Why are some women afraid to admit they are angry? Some fear they will be perceived as bad. They fear rejection by others, the church, and God. They never have learned to love themselves as God does so that they can be honest about their feelings. Often we take pride in telling ourselves how good we are because we're not angry.

Well, What Can I Do When I'm Angry?

Now that you know anger in itself is not a sin, give yourself permission to admit to the world, "Yes, I am angry! But from this moment on I plan to do something about it." Below is a five-step plan you can use as the basis for coming up with your own, personalized method of handling your emotions, because sometimes only *you* know what works best for you.

Five-Step Plan to Handle Anger

1. **ADMIT** your anger. It may not be a sin . . . yet!
2. **AX** your reaction. Cut your quick reactions to a much slower response. Train yourself to stop (breathe), drop (inside yourself), and roll (with the punches).

3. **ASK** yourself what the focus of your anger is. Is it real injustice that warrants some action . . . or am I angry because life isn't fair or things aren't as I'd like them to be?

4. **ANALYZE** your options. Do I have control over this situation or not? If I can do something, I will. If not, I will let go. Do I still hold *unrealistic expectations*? Do I need to set and enforce *boundaries*?

5. **ACT.** If you need to rebuke someone, learn to do it in love, without shaming. If you need to set or enforce boundaries, learn healthy ways to protect yourself and your family. Acting also may mean simply letting go and doing nothing.

Remember, anger is rooted in fear that injustice will prevail, that we won't get what we need or want, that life is not fair, or that we will be rejected again. Fear, simply put, is a lack of faith.

*W*hat Does My Fear Say?

People are going to keep hurting my kids or me. I'm going to have to fight to get what I want. I don't deserve this! I want life to be different; I want life to be fair.

*W*hat Does My Faith Say?

Life is not fair . . . but God is. People will try to hurt my children and me, but I can learn to protect myself and I can teach the children, too. I can change my attitude and let go of the anger. He can show me how.

Love Letter

DAUGHTER,

Why do you weep? Don't you know that even the sun and moon will be darkened, and there will be times when you just can't see? This is one of those seasons. Getting through this valley will take time and effort, but don't worry. I will provide all the grace you need and I am here with you. Before your feet stumble on the darkening hills, take my hand and hold tight.

Your Loving Father

7

Depression

*O*utside my window the morning sun rose slowly, painting pink and coral over the Santa Rosa mountains, while two ruby-throated robins perched in the palm trees, began singing their desert song. Inside my dark, stuffy bedroom I kept my eyes closed and buried my head deeper into the sweaty pillow and unwashed sheets. I didn't want to get up, so I didn't.

Drifting in and out of restless sleep, my mind raced until I couldn't stop, so I finally threw back the rumpled covers and stumbled out the bedroom door. I was sick of the nightmares and needed to distract myself so the thoughts would stop. "*Okay, I'll make coffee,*" I thought. While the pot perked, I stood in front of the hallway mirror and stared at myself. I recited out loud, like a schoolgirl's taunt, "No make up, greasy hair . . . guess what world, *I don't care!*" I laughed bitterly at myself and stuck my stomach out as far as I could, sloped my shoulders down like a Neanderthal woman and grunted "You're *fat!*" I stared. The reflection just looked back silently, and I added, "You're ugly and no one wants you! *No one!*"

As if it agreed with me, I heard the coffeepot start to sputter, but I didn't care. I dragged myself back to my room, plopped on my bed, stared at the ceiling, and thought of all I had to do. I was behind at work, the trash had piled up, I hadn't done laundry in weeks, nor had I showered or brushed my teeth in two days.

Feeling a little guilty about that, I got back up and headed to the kitchen. I stopped briefly at the mirror again and spat out snidely, "You're P-A-T-H-E-T-I-C!"

My girlfriends had been calling and inviting me out, but I didn't want to see or be with anyone. For hours I alternated between self-pity and outrage, until I finally got cleaned up later that afternoon. Then I just started counting the hours until bedtime. I wanted to cry, but couldn't.

I was turning my anger inward. I was upset with myself for making such poor choices in the beginning of our relationship, but I also was angry at the tuxedoed man who had stood in front of the church promising to love me, support me, and cherish me forever. If I had vented my anger to him, I—and the world—would have considered myself a witch. I also had to be nice to him because without his cooperation, I was afraid I'd never see my beloved little stepson again. Besides, I had loved and been deeply committed to my husband, and part of me didn't want to be nasty to the man who'd been my soul mate. I also prided myself on being a good person who wouldn't get angry at anyone. So because of *pride, fear,* and *wanting to stay in control,* I stuffed my tremendous anger down as deep as I could, until it forced its way back up through nightmares and depression. When it finally erupted, the ugly, stinking anger that had festered into bitterness was directed at someone *very precious*—me.

Depression Is Anger without Energy

When we understand that anger, a normal human response and also part of God's nature, can be expressed and dealt with in healthy ways, we can learn to change our habits of either feeding it and attacking others (outward) or stuffing it (inward). It's not hard to recognize anger when it's expressed outwardly, but when it goes underground, it becomes depression, or more simply *anger turned inward.*

Anger is like a firecracker. The same energy that explodes outward can implode inside of us, creating a vacuum that literally pulls our mental, emotional, and spiritual energy into a black hole. On the Fourth of July have you ever seen those fireworks that blast off into the air and are suppose to burst open but don't? As children we called them duds. I remember lighting them, and they fizzled, popped, sparked, and bounced around on the ground a little, but then just lay there. They weren't made like the other fireworks. Whatever was supposed to make all that energy burst open just ate away at the inside instead. After divorce, some of us become duds.

Emotional and Biochemical Depressions

If you're like me, you study the newsstands while you're in line at the store. Month after month women's magazines have articles on depression. Every year, publishers release more and more books about different types of depression, and plenty of up-to-date Web sites and other resources address the subject. As divorced women, we need to understand that a lot of our depression is due to our internalized anger at the loss and rejection, but it can result from others factors as well.

Most of us understand that our physical body is separate from, but one with, our mind and emotions. Depression can be *emotional,* which can in turn, affect and upset the healthy *chemical* balance of the body. When we stay in a depressed state for long periods after a divorce, our body may either be depleted of or start to produce chemicals that can keep us "stuck" feeling depressed. Then it's a vicious cycle. This is called "emotional depression" but it eventually can involve the body as well.

On the other side, "biochemical depression" is often genetic and can be triggered by nonemotional causes, but still results in chemical imbalance. When that happens, our emotions may fall into a depressed state. Think about it this way: When you have a nasty head cold, you eventually feel emotionally drained, too. Even though your life is just fine, staying in bed for three days can make anyone feel depressed. Mind and body influence each other.

Either way, experts agree that treatment for depression sometimes involves medication, but not always. For those who benefit from medication, reaching full health also requires working on their mental and emotional issues.

How Do I Know I Am Depressed?

In recent years the term depression has covered a wide range of separate, individual, negative emotions and is evidenced in just as many behaviors. Put a check by the ones you have experienced:

- ☐ Feeling out of sync with the world, others, and my normal routine
- ☐ Lack of energy/lethargy
- ☐ Emotional numbness/not caring
- ☐ Social withdrawal
- ☐ Insomnia
- ☐ Excess sleeping
- ☐ Crying
- ☐ Abnormal fatigue
- ☐ Daily feelings of worthlessness or guilt
- ☐ Difficulty concentrating
- ☐ Recurring feelings of hopelessness or helplessness
- ☐ More than minimal weight loss or gain
- ☐ Impaired reflexes
- ☐ Substance abuse
- ☐ Recurrent thoughts of death
- ☐ Suicide attempts
- ☐ Obsession/anxiety

- [ ] High sensitivity to criticism and rejection
- [ ] Mood swings
- [ ] Restlessness
- [ ] Agitation
- [ ] Irritability/anger
- [ ] Becoming overly active or overly sexual

Some Basic Facts

Here are some basic facts about depression:

- Depression is not a disease; it's a symptom of deeper, underlying mental, emotional, and/or medical issues.
- Depression can be part of the natural grieving process.
- Depression isn't always marked by sadness or crying.
- Depression can build quietly for years, with divorce only punctuating it.
- People with a natural temperament toward perfection or worry are more prone to depression than those who are optimists or who can let go more easily.
- Both assertive and passive personalities can be depressed, either internalizing or externalizing it, or both.
- Sometimes just catching up on sleep can help.
- Medical illness can cause depression.
- Depression suppresses the immune system and can trigger many other illnesses.
- Depression can recur, especially if we only treat it medically, never doing the deeper psychological work to heal emotional hurts, fears, and anxieties.
- Depression is contagious. It draws everyone in the family into the pit.
- Depression is often marked by an ongoing preoccupation with self.

- Depression is real, it's not imagined or all in your head.
- Depression can be cured.

Many divorced women I counsel have told me that depression is the greatest obstacle they've had to overcome. Julie described her feelings this way: "After my divorce, depression was probably the most difficult thing to work through, and I still suffer from it after fourteen years. The depression encompassed so many different things, and that is probably why it has been so difficult to work through. I felt like a failure for a long time. If only I had tried harder and been a different or better person. Even after I recognized that I could not have done anything more to make this marriage a success, the feelings still persisted."

How can someone still be depressed after fourteen years? Julie may be the personality type that tends to fear and worry. Unless she challenges herself to change her basic, underlying focus on life, she may get easily drawn back into a cycle of depression. Julie might have seriously worked on her anger and other negative emotions following her divorce, but when other unrelated negative circumstances arise, she may habitually revive old feelings from the divorce, adding them like old fuel on a new fire. Depression can be made up of layers of feelings, part of which Julie worked on and part of which remain repressed.

Julie also might be chemically stuck in depression and need the help of medication, a better diet, rest, and/or exercise. Some women who are depressed over divorce issues, hide in the cave of isolation that in itself creates a different depression. Sometimes they gain excessive weight that keeps them depressed, no matter how well they've handled other negative emotions.

Another reason women like Julie have a hard time recovering after fourteen years is that they simply refuse to let go of the bitterness.

Darlene also had a hard time getting over the dark period. She shares, "When I was first struggling with the question of whether or not to divorce my husband, I looked in bookstores for something that would help me understand my pain. All the books seemed to come from one direction—that divorce was excusable *only* for adultery or abandonment. Nothing helped me deal with the less obvious emotional, sexual, and spiritual abuse. This only sent me deeper into depression. The internal struggle was excruciating."

Darlene's depression seems to have been less about anger than about her struggle with guilt. Remember the stages of grieving? Once Julie and Darlene got past the shock and denial, they stayed stuck in *anger, guilt, and grief,* processing these emotions over and over. Unless they can get to the emotional tumor that's feeding the negative emotions, they may stay stuck for another fourteen years!

What Can I Do to Feel Better?

We are living in a time of great expectations and bitter disappointments. When things don't go our way, we get cranky or crabby—nice little words for anger. Today we prefer to call ourselves stressed because it sounds better than being angry. But how am I to get beyond this stage? How can I feel better? The first step is to stop the denial and admit that we have emotional anger and the next step is identifying the different challenges that we face because of our different personalities.

The *passive personality* struggles with admitting she's angry. She has had many angry people in her life, and she almost takes pride in being peaceful and quiet and *not* like them. Tending to be the victim of circumstances or other people's problems, she keeps her emotions inside, is self-protective, tired, worn down, and hopeless. She may tend to pick the easiest way out and focus solely on medications. She's predisposed to procrastination, and that can drag her depression out even further. If she's somewhat of a perfectionist, she'll find it doubly hard to even try to work through the emotional steps of healing depression; it's too hard, takes too much time, and, if she can't do it perfectly, why try? If she is fun-loving, she'll tend to stay depressed because not only is it too hard, the healing process is no fun! Her challenge will be to get up off the emotional couch, take action, and quit playing the martyr.

The *assertive personality* thinks she has it altogether and will tend to deny weakness or rush through the healing process, only to find herself down again in the future. Proud and self-sufficient, she has difficulty reaching out to others for help, tries to do it all herself, and even leaves God out of the process. If she's also part perfectionist, she'll have a hard time admitting the full extent of her emotional issues. She'll throw herself into recovery but forgets who's really in charge. Assertive women will take medication because it will hasten the healing, or they will avoid it, seeing it as a crutch or even as a lack of faith. If well-meaning people in the church have told her that medication for depression is bad, she might not even get help from a doctor. The assertive and fun-loving woman will do better in giving herself permission to laugh once in awhile, but she'll tend to not finish the work required for full emotional healing, stopping when it's no longer fun. Her challenge will be to slow down, embrace her weakness, and seek outside help.

Band-Aids for the Soul

We label some healing techniques as Band-Aid therapy because they do not really get to the core issues of our problems and full healing does not occur. But Band-Aids serve a useful purpose: they can stop the immediate bleeding and make us feel better right away. I always liked those colored Band-Aids with stars and hearts. No matter what your personality, you can start to feel a little better with these Band-Aids:

- Count your blessings. Thank God for your privileges. Climb back up in the Father's lap and take a deep breath.
- See a doctor to rule out biochemical problems that could be making your depression worse.

- Make a list of everything that makes you feel angry, sad, guilty, shameful, hopeless, or powerless. Take that list to a counselor.
- Start some form of fun exercise, such as walking, swimming, or dancing.
- Rework your budget so that you're not always stressed.
- Rework your schedule to provide more fun time, alone time, prayer time.
- Listen to beautiful, soothing, or upbeat music every day.
- Force yourself to socialize, even if you don't feel like it. Start with something simple, such as lunch with a girlfriend.
- Break up your routine. Go see a movie by yourself.
- Rent a funny video. *Houseboat* with Goldie Hawn is one of my favorites.
- Buy someone a small gift (depression is very self-focused).
- Move your furniture around or clean out your closet.
- Learn to set healthy boundaries so you are not a victim.
- Quit keeping secrets.
- Learn to be willing to lose in order to win.
- Sit down and write God a letter, pouring out your heart.
- Eat chocolate (I prefer dark).

Phony Joy

Florence Littauer tells the story of her son, Fred, a natural Melancholy personality and the opposite of his mother's cheerful, sunny Sanguine personality. "While I've always had the tendency to see the flowers in life, little Freddie grew up seeing the weeds. He looked so often at the negative side of things I finally announced to him one day that from now on I wanted him to start developing some phony joy because it was a lot better than genuine depression!"

Many people will try to change you after divorce, forcing you to have some phony joy because they are tired of your depression. You might even choose to put on that happy mask yourself, so that people will not further reject you. Phony joy may be a step, but it is not the answer. Rather, you can start to heal a layer at a time, recognizing that depression is just an outward sign of other very specific emotions that need to be addressed: shock, anger, fear, grief, guilt, and loneliness.

Dr. Les Carter, Ph.D., a counselor on the DivorceCare video series, is coauthor with Dr. Frank Minirth, M.D. in *The Freedom from Depression Workbook*. I still use that book once in a while since it helped me understand what was going on with my emotions in simple, easy terms. The book's twelve steps to managing depression are perfect if you want to take a slow, steady pace toward understanding and healing over the next twelve months or so. Dr. Carter advises that all it takes is "an inquisitive mind and a willingness to challenge your old ways of responding to problems."[1]

A word of caution, though: honoring your depressed feelings does not mean staying stuck in them for years, or using them as an excuse to remain a victim or to recycle your bitterness. There's something to be said about sometimes forcing yourself to wash your face, put on fresh lipstick, and look at the flowers instead of the weeds.

Even phony joy can be the first step in helping to heal a broken heart.

What Does My Fear Say?

I'm afraid that life will only get worse. I'm often afraid that I will never be financially secure or loved, or that life will be easy again. What if I have to work hard for the rest of my life or never have the things I wanted, hoped for, or dreamed of? What if no one wants me? I feel powerless, hopeless, and angry at the same time.

What Does My Faith Say?

My Father knows my needs. He never would allow me to go through dark times without the comfort of knowing he's right there. He's got all the tools I need to get through this tough time. I can acknowledge my feelings as temporary and every day take one step toward his outstretched hand.

Love Letter

PRECIOUS ONE,

Failing doesn't mean you are a failure, it means you haven't succeeded in everything yet. It doesn't mean you've accomplished nothing, it means you can learn something valuable. Failure doesn't mean you have been disgraced; it means you were willing to try but didn't have the tools or know-how to use them. It's never too late, Sweetheart. I will teach you.

Your Loving Father

8

Guilt

The Samaritan woman walked gracefully toward Jacob's well. Her olive skin was browned by the sun, and her long hair was plaited with colorful leather ties. Gold and silver rings glistened as her hands lowered the large clay pot from her shoulders to the ground. She'd already noticed the young Jewish rabbi who rested in the noontime shade, and she averted her gaze in respect. She could feel his eyes on her, but she went quietly about her business, taking the cover off her jar. As she began to draw the water, Jesus walked over to her, sat at the edge of the well, and asked, "Will you give me a drink?"

A mixture of fear, curiosity, and female pride rushed through her as she wondered why a Jew would even talk to a much-hated Samaritan, much less speak in a kind and friendly voice. A man is a man, she thought, and so she smiled warmly in her usual charming way and challenged the young Rabbi.

"You are a Jew, and I am a Samaritan woman," she said, turning to face him squarely, planting her feet firmly in the sand, hands on hips. "How can *you* ask *me* for a drink?" When Jesus laughed and nodded in agreement, she was immediately put at ease. He looked straight into her eyes, and she did not look away. His gaze was intent and he spoke to her as an equal. Other men usually only saw her exterior, but this man seemed to see inside her. An odd thing happened. In a voice of authority, the rabbi began to speak to her about living water. She sat down next to him, so close they almost touched. She felt unafraid and asked him questions, wanting to hear all he had to say. She'd always honored the God of her fathers and wanted to know more about these spiritual matters. As Jesus spoke, she grew excited and asked humbly, "Sir, give *me* this water!" She wasn't ready for his reply. "Go, get your husband, and then come back."

Without thinking, her shoulders slumped and she sighed. Most women enjoyed the protection of a loving husband who stayed with them for a lifetime. She hadn't been so lucky. Her first husband was a charmer and had swept her off her feet, but after a few years he left in the middle of the night to join a group of traveling merchants. In her grief over being abandoned, she consoled herself when the town blacksmith proposed. Everyone pressured her to marry him, saying, "He will take care of you." So she did. When she found her new husband in bed with someone else, she drifted from rage to depression so that he grew tired of her and divorced her. Over the years she'd continued to enter relationships with men who seemed wonderful at first, but who would abuse her either outwardly or by neglecting her. After the first few divorces, she grew accustomed to being outcast, and found it easy to leave on her own when a relationship deteriorated. Because women had few legal or financial rights, she'd quickly remarry for protection and acceptance in the community.

Over the years she failed to stop long enough to determine why she was stuck in these relationship patterns. Emotionally drained but determined nonetheless, she'd thought it was easier to move on. Even though her heart still ached for someone to love her, she'd resigned herself to her shame.

Now, somehow she trusted this man whose eyes held hers. She hated to admit the truth, fearing one more judgmental rebuke, but decided to open up. Choking back her embarrassment, she finally replied, "Sir, I *have* no husband."

In their culture, men did not approach or touch single women in public, but Jesus reached out and did what no man, Samaritan or Jew, had ever done. He took both of her hands in his, as a loving father might, and said tenderly, "You are right when you say you have no husband."

His eyes told her that he knew her pain and confusion. As he held her hands she felt that he'd seen those dark nights when she tossed and turned in guilt and regret, the days when others had humiliated her. Another woman might sympathize with her, but here was a man who seemed to know how badly she'd always wanted a husband she could count on, a man of integrity, a man of his word. No one had ever understood her so well. She could feel her emotions rising in her chest.

"You have had five husbands, and the man you have now is not your husband."

How did he know that? Was he a prophet? Somehow he knew the sordid truth about her failures, and yet he did not seem to be casting her aside in judgment, like the others had. His voice told her that he knew her frustration at so many failed marriages. He knew how she felt about having to live with a man just for protection, to avoid being alone, and the fear she had about ever risking marriage again.

"You have spoken truly," he said, nodding in approval at her honesty and willingness to be real with him.

She took a deep breath and sighed. She'd opened up and shared a very intimate part of her life, perhaps the most painful, and he knew already, he *understood!* She sat there quietly listening, unaware of the others at the well and forgetting about her own plans for the day. She wanted to know more.

Jesus told her about his Father. As he spoke, she was convicted of her failures but felt her guilt and shame melt away. She came to understand that her search for love with a husband had impeded her search for something even richer. Jesus's words made her resolve to make changes in her life. "I know the Messiah is coming!" she shared excitedly, as if to tell him she accepted and believed everything he'd been telling her. She could hardly believe it when he looked her in the eye and said, "I who speak to you am he."

With that, Jesus's disciples, who had returned, approached them, wondering what had been going on. The Samaritan woman, overcome with joy, leaned forward, hugged Jesus tightly, and grinned. A quick hug, because of her eagerness to run out and tell others, and perhaps because of those who were standing around watching. Maybe Jesus hugged her back, held her face in her hands, and said with a smile, "Hey, what about that drink?"

Scripture tells us she completely forgot about her jar and ran off to share the exciting news. I'm sure the woman at the well thought about the young rabbi all the way home that afternoon. Even though she was still divorced, her steps must have been lighter and her shoulders stronger as she realized she'd left her guilt, sorrow, and bitterness at the well and was, indeed, carrying back living water.[1]

Lessons Learned at the Well

After the shock and denial of divorce wears off, the first thing many of us do is look back and question ourselves. What could we have done better? What was our fault in the matter? Where did we go wrong? What will others say? Is God mad at us? Is it too late?

I asked myself all those questions. Because of my husband's failings, I easily could have blamed everything on him, and any outsider would have agreed with me. But more than staying "guilt free" I wanted to embrace the truth. In truth, we faced huge obstacles from the very beginning, which I had seen and ignored. I thought they would not matter, or I could change things or control the situation for the good. I failed by giving into the powerful emotional need for, and almost dogged pursuit of, a husband and family instead of making choices God's way.

In wanting to create the perfect family, I tried to project my own values onto Tom. I saw a man with a troubled past and a hurting soul, and I became his rescuer. I suggested, advised, counseled, reminded, and begged him to become the husband and father of my storybook dreams. I didn't respect his need, and God's desire for him, to find his own path. In the name of encouragement, I pushed him to become something he did not want to become. Our marriage pattern was my pushing and his pulling away.

Thankfully, in counseling I'd learned some powerful principles about failure and guilt that kept me from chaining myself in an emotional dungeon and throwing away the key. In his book *Rejection Junkies*, Dr. Gary Lawrence teaches the difference between false guilt and genuine guilt:

- False guilt is an anxiety created from a fear of being rejected for lack of performance. For example, I feel guilt and shame when I tell people I have been divorced because I assume they will think less of me and judge me. In some way or another I will not measure up, fit in, or belong. Because I have not performed the way they expect, I anticipate their rejection. With false guilt we feel like we failed, usually based on someone else's expectations.
- Genuine guilt is a grieving created by the Holy Spirit over a situation. I feel genuine guilt for the times I failed to be honest in the relationship, attacked my spouse's character, was stubborn, or took the easy way out. I regret some actions that I took and some I did not. We experience genuine guilt when we know we failed to trust and follow God.[2]

The Facts about Failure

I also learned that *just because I failed does not mean I am a failure*. David failed, Solomon failed, and Paul failed. Count yourself lucky . . . Peter had *his* failures recorded four times in the world's most read book. Great men and women of God who were deeply loved and used by him failed countless times. Failure is part of being human. I know that until the day I die I will fail and fail and fail and fail . . . and fail again. But I will never let that stop me from trying my best and knowing I am still deeply and passionately loved by my Heavenly Father.

What should you do with your failure? Own it, seek forgiveness for it, speak honestly about it when appropriate, and learn from it. Remember, we all fail, but we don't need to stay down.

Shame and Guilt

Kim sent me an email that read, "My most difficult issue has been the shame of being a twice-divorced Christian. There is a stigma from society, from church members, and from myself. I'm embarrassed and full of guilt feelings." Kim feels shame from the rejection she's felt from others and herself, and her perceived rejection by God.

Yet, God does not reject Kim nor us. He rejects our sinful actions, but never us. When we know we did something wrong, we will feel genuine guilt, but we need not carry shame. Shame is the feeling that not only did we do something wrong, we are something wrong; we are unworthy, pathetic, useless, rotten, and sinful. It's true that human nature is tainted, but when we forget the power of God's forgiveness, love, acceptance, and grace, we insult him.

How Unresolved Guilt Hurts Us and Our Families

Unresolved guilt feelings can keep us in emotional bondage to our ex-spouse and even our children. To try to make up for the past, we can spend the rest of our lives trying to be nice and making life easier as restitution for our guilt. Instead of restitution, however, behavior motivated by guilt creates unhealthy relationships. We stuff our anger toward a still-abusive ex-spouse because being nice and being angry can't coexist. Or we go overboard in giving the kids too much, or relax the firm boundaries they need because we want them to feel good and to love us.

Marsha is a perfect example of someone bound up by guilt after a divorce. Her ex-husband, Ed, was a poor provider, rarely paid attention to her needs, and was unfaithful with a woman at his work. Fed up with years of an empty marriage and now the affair, Marsha divorced Ed and tried not to look back. But the guilt haunts her whenever someone asks, "Did you two go to counseling to try to make it work?" Ed had sought her forgiveness and begged her to give him one more chance, but Marsha had made up her mind; no counseling, no second chance, no more pain for her.

Her three children miss their dad, though, and Marsha feels guilty. Deep down she suspects she should have stayed and given it one more chance. But Ed remarried, so now it's too late. Ed is still unreliable, failing to pay child support and showing up late to pick up the kids or to bring them home on weekends. But Marsha doesn't push. She lets Ed have unstructured time with the children with no financial accountability. Unfortunately, her anger at the lack of boundaries in the relationship keeps her emotionally tied to him.

Marsha also lets her children stay up to all hours, eat what they want, and even talk back to her disrespectfully, because she does not want to yell at them or make them unhappy. She thinks taking them away from their father has hurt them enough. She doesn't want to add any more misery to their lives. Sadly, the children *are* miserable because their mom is letting guilt stand in the way of her teaching, challenging, and holding her children accountable for loving, mature behavior.

How do you stop guilt from keeping you tied up with others? Start with seeking forgiveness from God, your ex, the kids, and anyone else who has you dancing to their tune. Ask God to forgive you for nursing that guilt and not releasing it. Ask your ex to forgive you for your attitudes of fear, failure, or bitterness toward him. Tell him you will still treat him with respect, but you will no longer live in guilty fear or bondage to him. Ask the kids to forgive you, if they are old enough to understand, for failing to lead, teach, and guide them properly. Explain how guilt got in your way. Teach them that guilt is meant to convict us to repentance, but not to keep us stuck. Let the kids know that guilt should be with us only for a short while and once we've sought and received forgiveness, it's over!

Damaged Goods

If you feel like damaged goods, replace that false guilt with this thought: Having been through the problems and pain of marriage and divorce at least once, you have gained wisdom that never-divorced people don't have. Should you be blessed with a new marriage partner, you can ride shotgun while he drives the team of horses through the desert. Since you've been this route before, you can scout the surrounding terrain, knowing what to look for: the winding turns, the steep paths, and the signs and sounds of trouble ahead. Think of yourself in new terms, as did the women at the well. You will be an invaluable partner in the journey, a comrade-in-arms, a true helpmate.

Jesus offered the Samaritan women living water not so much because she needed to be cleaned up after the huge mess she called her life, but because she needed the refreshing, soothing, healing powers of his love, forgiveness, acceptance, and grace. You can have that living water, too.

What Does My Fear Say?

I'm a failure. I know all the areas in which I was wrong but it's too late to go back and fix them. I'm tired of trying to make up for my mistakes to others, but I guess it will never end. I know God must hate me; why else would I feel so miserable?

What Does My Faith Say?

God does not hate me; he loves me! He hates where I have failed, but he forgives and forgets. I can take a lesson from him and let go. I can choose to own my genuine guilt, let go of false guilt, seek forgiveness, and move on. I can bathe myself in his living water.

Love Letter

DAUGHTER,

Do not worry about your life. Don't worry about food, clothes, or money. Don't worry about the children, your ex-husband, his family, or your friends. It's normal for you to have fears, but I want you to change the way you respond to them. As soon as you are aware of a fear, will you replace it with your faith in me? Will you seek me first instead of trying to figure it all out on your own or ignoring it and letting it overwhelm you?

I have a promise for you. Seek me first and I will make sure you have everything you need.

Your Loving Father

9

Fear

As she was leaving the examining room, a sick woman turned to her doctor and said, "Doctor, I am afraid to die. Tell me what lies on the other side."

With a laugh the doctor said, "Well, since I haven't been there myself, I can't tell you details."

The woman didn't smile. Sensing her uneasiness, he continued, "I do know God promises it will be wonderful, with no pain or sickness, and certainly nothing to fear."

"That's easy for you to say, doctor" the woman replied, still not convinced. "I've read about heaven since I was a little girl and intellectually I have no problem with it. I'm having trouble with my emotions, I think. Maybe I have faith in my head but not in my heart. I don't know." The woman sighed.

The doctor put his arm around the woman and walked her along the office corridor.

"Maybe I can tell you a story that will help," he said.

"When we went on vacation last summer, I went ahead to open the beach house we'd rented, and my wife and children followed two days later with Buster, our family dog. Buster's a cute little fella, been with us since he was a puppy. Well, when they drove up and my wife and children started unpacking their things from the car, Buster ran up the steps and started scratching the front door. He'd never been to that beach, much less that cottage. He had no idea what was on the other side of the door, but he could hear my voice on the other side. He knew it was safe. When I opened the door he leapt up into my arms and started licking my face."

The woman started to smile, understanding the doctor's story. He finished by saying,

"I have no idea what heaven is really like, but I know my Master is there, and I have no reason to fear. When the door opens, I will pass through, knowing he is waiting for me with open arms."

Fear Is Simply a Lack of Faith

After my divorce I was overcome with fears. I worried (another name for fear) that the house would go into foreclosure, that I could not support myself financially, and that I'd never have a happy marriage, ever. I was afraid I would not get to continue my relationship with my stepson and that society would see me as a failure. I was *anxious* about many things. I remembered, though, that Gerald Jampolsky had written in his book, *Love Is Letting Go of Fear*, that life consists of only two basic human emotions: love and fear.[1]

Think about it. Every negative emotion is rooted in some form of fear. Our anger usually is rooted in fear we won't get our way or that injustice will prevail. When we're depressed, we fear that we have no power or that things will not get brighter. Stress, worry, and anxiety are all based on fear of loss, fear of rejection, fear of abandonment, fear of powerlessness, fear of being used, fear of our children being hurt, fear of failure, fear of hard work . . . *fear, fear, fear!*

Neil Anderson states it quite simply in *Victory Over the Darkness*: "If fear is controlling your life then faith is not."[2]

I used to get irritated with that statement because I have had faith since I was a child. But then I learned about the constant battle in our heads between *what we know* and *how we feel*. It's not that we don't have faith, but sometimes faith stays in our head and the fear takes over our heart. Have you ever felt like this?

I *know* God loves me, but sometimes I don't *feel* like he does.
I *know* I can make it with his grace, I just don't *feel* like I will.
I *know* he would never leave me, it just *feels* like he's not here.
I *know* the kids will be all right, I just don't *feel* like they will.

Overcoming fear can be as easy as stopping and reminding ourselves of some basic facts, which we probably already believe on an intellectual level:

I know God loves me and has a plan for me.
He will never leave me.
He will never reject me.
He knows all my needs before I do.
He hears me; he understands me.
He promises to meet all my needs if I put him first.
He has not given me a spirit of fear.
If fear is overtaking me, all I have to do is call on him.

Make a commitment today to start being aware of how your emotions can take control over what you know to be true. Faith is living based on what we know, not just how we feel.

When Fear Is a Good Thing

Fear serves a good purpose. It alerts us to situations that might require our immediate attention. It warns us that we might have a part to play in solving a problem. If I fear losing my home, I might have to re-do my budget and start looking for new housing. The kids might have to stop taking piano lessons so I can afford the dentist. I might have to swallow my pride and ask for help. I might have to make changes in my life to remove stress and anxiety. After

I take the steps I can, or reach out for the help I need, I must let go of any residual fear, because it no longer serves any useful purpose.

Without fear, we could not have courage. Courage is the ability to accept your fears as normal but face them anyway, in faith.

What do you fear? We often avoid the word fear, thinking it sounds weak and wimpy. We replace it with words such as anxiety, worry, and concern, which make us sound like deeply caring women. If we want to heal from divorce, however, we must stop fooling ourselves and get gut-wrenching, knuckle-cracking, soul-baring *honest*.

When I have an intense emotional reaction (tight chest, furrowed brow, tears, anger . . . you know the rest) to anything or anyone, I stop and say, "Okay, Rose, what does your fear say, and what does your faith say?" It gets me right back on track. It helps me hear my Master's voice and pass right through that door.

What Does My Fear Say?

Among a million other things, I'm afraid of being hurt, used, abandoned again, taken advantage of, getting ripped off in court, losing the kids' loyalty, having others believe the lies, having to work too hard, being alone, and not being forgiven by God. Sometimes I am outraged with fear; other times I am paralyzed by it.

What Does My Faith Say?

My Master is right here, all the time. I have nothing to fear. If I do feel afraid, I will examine my fears and take any necessary action. Then I will let my fears pass, knowing that my emotions are temporary and fleeting, but God's faithfulness stands forever.

Love Letter

DEAR ONE,

Can you hear my voice? I know you are lonely, but I want you to come and stay with me. I am with you and will watch over you wherever you are and whatever you do. I will never leave you until I have done what I have promised you.

Your Loving Father

10

Loneliness

Most of us know that loneliness shows up at night after the kids go to bed, but it can hit the hardest at unexpected times and even in a room full of people: at the office Christmas party, the weekend church service, or in a dark movie theatre. One of the loneliest times for me is when I have exciting news to share, but when I call everyone I know, no one is home. Another is when I come home and no one greets me with a hug.

I asked some of the divorced women I know to describe their loneliness and the first reply I received was from Gina, divorced and just separated from a new relationship. "I had the worst attack of loneliness this weekend. It was torturous. The volcano erupted, the tidal wave and earthquake hit, and the all-time heart-break zoomed out of control. After hours and hours of crying, I'm at my end. I just can't do this alone. I'm forty-four years old, no partner, no kids, no significant family (except my mom) and no single friends. Everyone is married—everyone! I am sick of eating alone, sleeping alone, and being alone. I'm scared and frightened and not sane anymore."

Janie, recently divorced, hates even going to work. "Everyone, and I mean everyone, has a special someone, whether or not they are married. It's not fair! The only people who are alone and lonely are the homely ones, the rejects, and I sure don't fit in with them!"

For Mary, divorced ten years, the nights were the loneliest. "I still just lie there, thinking how empty my bed is. I think of my ex-husband and how he used to feel and smell. Then I think of him with his new wife. It's hell."

Sophia says, "I can't settle down. I walk around my new place picking things up and putting them down. I clean out drawers. I stay so busy that I can't go to sleep."

Blanca uses her children to stay busy and lick the loneliness. "I know I put way too much time into my children. Sounds funny, doesn't it, since we think kids should come first. It might seem good for them, but it's bad for me. I need space and time and friends of my own. Maybe if I did, I wouldn't be so crabby."

Some women don't have to deal with loneliness after divorce. At their jobs, they are surrounded by similarly educated and intelligent peers and coworkers. They have a close extended family, and at home their adorable children snuggle up to them and kiss them good night each evening. Their time alone in bed at night is a blessed relief from the hectic day of a noisy office and evenings with a houseful of kids. These women rarely get lonely, especially after years with an abusive or noncommunicative spouse.

Eva Marie wrote about her divorce more than twenty-five years ago, and her response is typical for many divorced women who were not happy during the marriage or who like their space. "Lonely when he left? No way. My biggest struggle was financial. He got to the bank before I did and left me with one dime. Literally. Back then you could do that. He had, shall we say, sexual identity issues and married me for social acceptance. There would be no children. My marriage was a farce and ended in violence. So the easiest thing to overcome was the absence of another human being in the house. I was blessedly free!"

Solitude Versus Loneliness

Many divorced women love being alone after divorce. Their hobbies, pets, kids, and careers keep them content. While they would be quite open to a new relationship, they are not actively pursuing it and are fine without it. However, some women who prefer aloneness still have a real emptiness, a longing for another husband, but not if pain accompanies him. Some hope for a new relationship but have little faith in finding it. Some want nothing to do with marriage, ever.

According to the *Baker Encyclopedia of Psychology and Counseling*, loneliness (as a clinical syndrome) is "marked by painful feelings of sadness or longing and almost always by the absence of, yet felt desire for, relationship with others."[1] We need to remember that loneliness:

- Can be the result of other's actions (as in death or divorce) or self-inflicted (when we isolate, withdraw, or fail to take action to connect emotionally)
- Often stirs up feelings of worthlessness and inadequacy
- Can serve as a primary source of depression
- May be a precursor to suicidal feelings
- Is not bound by time, with some passing through it quickly and others stuck there for years
- Can be due to a lack of a social network (social loneliness)
- Can occur within relationships that lack true emotional intimacy (emotional loneliness)

Solitude is different from loneliness in that it is not always marked by that anxious, sometimes all-consuming, desire for relationship. Aloneness provides a state free of the world's noise and distractions, in which we can gain insight and perspective into ourselves and our relationship with God. Healthy solitude is a place where we can be still and hear his voice. Being alone is different than being lonely, and unless we can clear our minds from all the layers of negative emotions that keep us in bondage, we will always be lonely.

itterness

If they were being honest, many of the women who tell me they do not want to remarry would admit they still carry a large load of unresolved hurts. They fear rejection, failure, and being abandoned again. Personalities also play a part in how we respond to loneliness:

Passive, quiet women who were outwardly abused and controlled often want nothing to do with men ever again and shut them out for good. Others who tend to be victims may seek another abuser, willing to trade the abuse for care and companionship.

Assertive women who had to assume leadership in their marriages because of a passive, unresponsive spouse also don't want another chain around their necks and don't seek new relationships. As independent as they are, however, some may start looking for a new husband out of plain, old-fashioned loneliness.

Many women remain single and fill their lives with enriching careers and service to others, finding a true level of contentment. Yet, not all women are meant to remain single. Sometimes staying single is a result of a quiet, bitter refusal to ever be hurt or used again, and of not knowing how to establish a healthy a relationship with a new partner. For some women it's just easier to stop hoping. When that happens, the root of bitterness has taken hold of their hearts. Women who have bitterness (anger, fear, or wounded spirits) will not be truly content whether or not they are in a relationship.

Loneliness is a national epidemic. In our world of fast cars, noisy TVs, and endless soccer, baseball, and ballet, we can stay distracted and busy from morning to night and never think we are lonely. Loneliness comes in degrees, and in certain areas. So even if you think you are not lonely, you might want to read further. Listen to some of the comments from divorced women who have written to me:

> "I'm about eighty percent content, I think. I'd like someone in my life to share the ups and downs with—could be another man or even a girlfriend who has more time than my married friends have. I think I am doing okay, but I'd love to remarry someday—after I finish finding myself again—not a wife, not Mom, just me." —*Karen*

Karen also told me she did not miss her ex-husband and, because he was not there for her during the marriage, she was lonely even being married.

Donna Cowan, who authored *The Single Solution,* shared the following with me in a personal conversation: "When am I most unhappy as a single? When I put myself in positions where there are couples everywhere—dances, parties, movies at night. I do things by myself all the time, but I do it during the day when you aren't as likely to find people out there strolling hand in hand, hugging, kissing and smooching, and making your green-eyed monster emerge from hibernation.

She added, "In the old days there was nothing that would stave my loneliness except going out and finding others. I was always at some club or another, dancing up a storm. Since the second divorce, spending time with my little daughter keeps me busy."

The Need to Belong

I'm the oldest of eight children. Growing up, each of us always had at least one friend over to play or spend the night, so as many as twenty people were eating, sleeping, making noise, and having fun in our home at one time. In my twenties and thirties, even though I had no children, I spent weekends at my three sisters' homes, feeding, bathing, loving, and even disciplining their kids. Though unable to be a biological mother, I felt I still belonged to a large family.

Years later and post-divorce, I had to face life as a middle-aged woman with no family of my own. Although I'd been a stepmom for nearly ten years, my "baby" was gone now, too. Because of where I live and work full time, I'm not even able to have a pet. Nearly all my thirty nieces and nephews are grown and have moved out on their own, and many of my siblings have moved away. I still would like to be part of a family, to fit in and belong, but I don't. My many friends are kind enough to include me on holidays, but I often feel like a third wheel. I understand every bit of the pain of loneliness that we women share.

I ofttimes thought something was wrong with me that I had such a strong need to belong. Then I came to understand God wired me that way. It's not wrong to feel lonely. He put that powerful urge inside us for a reason. I just didn't realize what it was.

The Meaning of Being Lonely

Even though I know only the first line, I love the Backstreet Boys's song on their album *Millennium:*

> "Show me the meaning of being lonely
> Is this the feeling I need to walk with
> Tell me why I can't be there where you are
> There's something missing in my heart"[2]

What is the meaning of being lonely? I've discovered that, like all emotions, it serves a purpose. Remember how fear tells us that some problem needs our serious attention? Loneliness signals us that we are out of relationship with God and ourselves. It indicates that we have placed relationships with others on a higher pedestal and have forgotten that all humans ultimately will abandon us in some way, whether they mean to or not. Loneliness reminds us that we have a need to belong, first to God. Through our loneliness, he wants to draw us closer. These seemingly negative circumstances serve to remind us we were made to belong, to him. *That's* the meaning of being lonely.

More Band-Aid Therapy?

We can rebuild a social network, join groups and clubs, throw ourselves into our children or work, even start dating again and still be heartbreakingly lonely. But nothing is wrong with taking practical steps to get and stay connected with others; these Band-Aids function quite well to help us feel better right away. Because of our unique temperaments and lifestyles, we each may find different temporary cures more effective in treating our loneliness, but the following seem to help most everyone:

- Get some help—professional or pastoral counseling doesn't have to cost a lot.
- Help others—staying focused on our own pain only serves to worsen it.
- Sit down and talk to God. Write him a letter. Get intimate with him.
- Wait it out—loneliness won't kill you.
- Do something you like—balance the pain with some pleasure.
- Read a book or buy a video about how to date the right way.
- Quit watching romantic movies for awhile—Don't torture yourself.

These remedial, quick-fix steps can provide some relief, but don't let them take the place of a deep, intimate relationship with the Father, who created us to be in love first *with him*.

Living Water (Again)

A respected college professor used a Mason jar and rocks to illustrate a principle about life's priorities and human nature. He arranged piles of large, medium, and small rocks on his desk and asked the students which rocks to put in first to fit the most in the jar. The students who put the smaller and medium-sized rocks in first were not able to fit in the larger rocks. Then the professor taught the class that by putting the biggest rocks in first, then medium and then smaller rocks, you could accommodate the most rocks and make sure you didn't miss the big important ones. Obviously, this illustrated how we can manage (or mismanage) our time and priorities.

Then he asked the students if any more rocks could fit in the already filled-to-the-brim jar. They all said no. The professor proceeded to pour very fine sand into the jar, filling up all the little cracks and crevices. The students learned that with the right approach we can keep fitting more and more things into our lives.

Sometimes we do the same thing to fill the void in our hearts. The big rocks are usually our children and our jobs, and medium rocks are housework, dinner, errands, sports. Little rocks and sand can be all the other millions of things we do in the day and into the evenings to avoid our feelings of loneliness, but there's still a void.

The professor had one more trick up his sleeve. He asked the class again if *anything* else could fit in the jar and they said, "No way!" Then he poured an entire cup of clear, cold water into the jar, which everyone had thought was full.

In that story I see another principle being illustrated. Even with our busy lives as single women and mothers, we still have room for living water. To avoid loneliness, we can overschedule ourselves to full, but God's love still can fill even the tiniest of holes that keep us feeling empty inside.

What Does My Fear Say?

My fear tells me I will be stuck in this painful place of lone-liness forever. I'm afraid I will never have anyone to lean on, to love, and to love me back. I'm worried that I will become even lonelier in my old age. What if no one ever wants to marry me? What if no one ever even wants to love me?

What Does My Faith Say?

I know I was created to draw close to my Heavenly Father and rest in his arms. My loneliness is temporary. I can take some steps to help the situation, and I know he can help me with the rest of my feelings. I will go to him and not wallow in self-pity.

Love Letter

My Child,

Get rid of all bitterness, rage, and anger. Let go of your hurts and come back to me. Put your hand back into mine once more. Let me wash you with my grace and fill you to over-flowing with my love.

Your Loving Father

~❧ 11 ❧~

Bitterness

Sweet-smelling grasses and pungent pine trees grow thick and green in the breathtakingly beautiful lakeside forests of Michigan's Upper Peninsula. Crystal blue lakes lie still and calm, while cool streams wind through flower-flecked meadows and wild apple orchards. No one would suspect that lurking just below the surface of this pretty postcard picture is the giant, life-sucking *armillaria bulbosa fungus*, one of the world's largest living organisms. The 1,500-year-old fungus, which has woven itself into the very fabric of the ecosystem over the centuries, covers over thirty-seven acres (more than five football fields), weighs in excess of one hundred tons (fifty cars), and is described by botanists as "roughly the texture of rotting fabric." Although most of the fungus lives underground, visible signs of it at the surface include tree rot and mushroom growth.

When I read about this in the newspaper, I thought it was the perfect word-picture to describe what bitterness does to our soul. We may be perfectly coifed, manicured, and fit. We may have saintly faces, perfect church attendance, and beautiful clothes with shoes to match. We might be wonderful mothers, the best of friends, and selfless volunteers in our communities, but just beneath our surface can hide the stinking, rotting root of bitterness.

Like the fungus, which eventually overtakes and kills, the bitterness that results from our divorce can invade and destroy our emotional, physical, and spiritual health. Headaches, sleeplessness, anxiety, weight problems, even cancer, and a myriad of other physical maladies can take hold of us when we harbor the root of bitterness. The health or relationship problems that we might think are unrelated to our divorce can actually be symptoms of a giant root of bitterness.

What Is Bitterness?

I used to think that bitterness was limited to an emotional feeling of anger, revenge, resentment, or unforgiveness. Not so! Because of my Sanguine personality, I don't hold onto anger and am quick to forgive—sometimes *too* quickly. I just want everyone to be friends again. Thus, the bitterness I usually have to battle is a wounded spirit. It's less hostile, but it eats away at my peace and joy nonetheless. Feelings of sorrow and hurt that linger too long are just as bitter as anger and rage.

Imagine a ripe peach on your kitchen counter. Its flesh can be bruised, the skin can be moldy, and fruit flies can be buzzing all around. All three factors diminish and ultimately destroy the sweetness of the fruit. So, too, the root of bitterness referred to in Hebrews 12:15 can take many different forms.

At the New Life Dynamics counseling center in Phoenix, Arizona, the staff teaches that bitterness is the negative feeling we nurse, including:

Resentment
A wounded spirit
Anxiety
Fear or guilt
Avoidance
A sense of loss or abandonment
A feeling of betrayal

Bitterness is an attitude of failing to rejoice in life and all it holds. It takes root when we fail to embrace our pain as part of the way God can work his wonders, show his magnificence, and bring us to greater character development. Bitterness flies in the face of what God has told us, to not seek revenge, worry, fear, or be sorrowful. It reflects a total lack of appreciation of his gifts.

Bitterness attaches itself to our vulnerable spots, feeds off our fears, worries, and anger, and separates us from God. It worms its way into our souls and spirits, and it even destroys our bodily vessels.

Bitterness says, "Sorry, God, I don't care that you will meet my needs and take care of me. I don't care that you have promised me help in time of need. I like being angry. I like feeling depressed. I like worrying and I am not ready to let go of these feelings!" Bitterness is completely self-focused, and over time it will consume us.

Sadly, bitterness keeps us fixated at the greatest point of our pain.

How We Can See Bitterness

You can see bitterness in people's faces and hear it in their tone of voice. They make angry, caustic comments, sling sarcasm around, or whine endlessly about their struggles. You can see corners of lipsticked mouths turned down just a little and dull pain in perfectly painted eyes.

Someone who never smiles is bitter. Someone who is withdrawn is bitter. A woman who is a perpetual victim is bitter. Workaholics, spendaholics, and "sleep-aholics" are bitter. Fast-talking, funny women even can be bitter. One of the worst forms of feminine bitterness is something we've all been guilty of—*male bashing.*

I don't know how many emails I get every day from female friends, especially those in unhappy marriages or who have been divorced, in which there are bitter attacks on men, thinly disguised as jokes. Surely you've heard (too many times) the riddle about the auto accident involving Santa Claus, the Perfect Woman, and the Perfect Man? The reader is asked to determine who was the single survivor of the car crash. The answer—The Perfect Woman, because there is no such thing as Santa Claus or the Perfect Man. I chuckled too, when I first heard it, but having learned to be sensitive to any trace of negative, bitter attitudes of my own, I felt a twinge of shame that we wounded women have resorted to such humor. Although some think me a stick-in-the-mud, I have asked all my friends not to send me any more male-bashing jokes or stories. A few jokes may be as small as one single sapling with fungus, but it could be the sign of a one hundred-ton root of bitterness.

Doesn't Divorce Give Me the Right to Be Bitter?

Too often we focus on our rights, not our responsibilities. We really have no right to anything in our world, including our life and the air we breath; they are *all* gifts from God. It is a privilege to be alive, to be healthy, to have children. It is our responsibility to respond to life the way God wants, and that means refusing to let the root of bitterness take hold.

What we think are rights are really just the normal human responses to life's tragedies. Bitterness results when we hold too long the normal emotion we feel after someone sins against us . . . or we perceive someone wronged us, even God. After a lifeless marriage or gut-wrenching divorce:

- We have a *right* to be angry, but a responsibility to either take required action or let go.
- We have a *right* to be hurt and wounded, but a responsibility not to wallow in our wounds.
- We have a *right* to be concerned about our children, homes, health, and finances, but a responsibility not to obsess over them.

Among the divorced women I've dealt with, some of the most common signs of bitterness are the anger, fear, hostility, and spirit of uncooperativeness with their ex-husband and his new spouse. Here are some examples of bitterness:

Lenora refused to let her young son have a special one-half hour visit with his noncustodial dad for ice cream one night, and she purposely withheld visitation the day of dad's baptism.

Claire is so worried that her children will love their new step-mom that she can't say enough bad things about her to her ex-husband and the children.

Nora stays depressed because she never has enough money so the kids have to do without many of the basics that other families have, such as a warm winter coat that fits right or a much-needed trip to the orthodontist.

Juanita, a powerful personality who wore the pants in her marriage, still demands to know where her ex-husband is, whom he's with, what he does with the kids on his weekends, and how much money he's spending. She's worried that she will lose the control over him that seemed to give her security before.

How to Get Rid of Bitterness

First, if you are bitter toward God in any way, admit it and ask him to forgive you for your attitude. Then ask him to forgive you for all the forms of bitterness you've had toward other people or things. *Know that* in Jesus, you are forgiven.

Then, make a list of everyone toward whom you still feel angry, hurt, wounded, fearful, jealous, and any other negative feelings that conflict with full peace, joy, love, and acceptance. This might include people from your past.

Now, invite your best girlfriend over for the day. (You need a close friend or relative who will understand and hold you accountable while you get rid of your bitterness.) With your friend sitting beside you, make a phone call to everyone on the list and ask forgiveness from them for your attitude. Start with your ex-husband.

You don't need to (and shouldn't) get into a long, drawn out discussion because that's not the purpose of your call. It's to humbly own your failings so that they no longer have power over you.

If someone says, "What on earth are you talking about?" you can respond "It's just that I've had the wrong attitude toward you, and I don't want to anymore. Will you please forgive me?"

Some people won't forgive you; some will try to draw you into an argument. Learn to say, "I don't want to get into a discussion; I simply want to apologize and seek your forgiveness." With hard cases you might have to repeat this a few times and then just politely hang up. Don't get bitter again. Remember they, too, are probably hurting, fearful, or angry.

Don't expect them to ask you for forgiveness for what they did to you. But if they do happen to ask, grant them the same forgiveness God gives you.

It can be scary, but in my counseling programs I have personally found that this simple process of being able to directly and openly unplug from these "emotional energy thieves" brings the most wonderful freedom imaginable. It was hard at first. I'll never forget calling my husband's ex-wife. She hated me, did everything she could to get her son to hate me, and had more than once threatened my life. When I asked her to forgive me for my attitude toward her, I felt she no longer had any power over me.

I called my parents, some of my adult siblings, and friends and asked them to forgive me for my bitterness toward them. When I did, I was free.

How to Avoid Bitterness

Keep reminding yourself that your loving Father will take care of every single one of your needs. Make it a mental habit so that the next time you suffer a rejection, a loss, a fear, or worry, you won't get emotionally sucked down by the fungus among us.

Make notes to yourself using this affirmation below, or any version that works for you. Put Post-it notes on the bathroom mirror, on the car, at your desk at work, or in your wallet. Tattoo it on your forehead if you have to!

Even though I might not feel like it today, I *know* God wants every good thing for me. He will use every bad circumstance to work for good in my life. He gives me hope and a promise to meet all my needs. I need not worry, fear, or be anxious about *anything*! I will be patient and wait for things to get better, because I refuse to be bitter.

What Does My Fear Say?

I know I'm bitter, but I just can't help it. So many bad things have happened to me. What if I stay bitter forever? What if I can't get the nerve to call people and seek forgiveness for my attitude toward them?

What Does My Faith Say?

God is with me always. He can sit right next to me, drenching me in his grace and his love and giving me the confidence to do what I need to do. He loves me so much I need not fear anyone's rejection!

Love Letter

MY DAUGHTER,

I know why you weep. Lay your head on me and let the tears fall onto my shoulder. Do you trust me? Listen to what I have to say and believe that I will turn your mourning into gladness (Jer. 31:13).

Your Loving Father

12

Grieving

Have your eyes ever been so puffy and swollen from crying they looked like freshly cut slits in rising dough? Has the skin under your nose been so raw from blowing and wiping with Kleenex that it feels like you'd been rubbing yourself with the cheese grater? That's how I felt the week I finally grieved the loss of my marriage, my stepson, and the family I had always dreamed of, pursued diligently, and lost in the end.

I'd been doing pretty well in the year following my divorce. I felt good, even happy about life in general, having worked steadily through most of my grief. Every once in awhile, though, I would still be overcome with tears or deep sadness. Like a pesky child who keeps trying to interrupt you when you're on the phone, my grief kept tugging at my heart. I decided if I was going to move on, I'd have to hang up my busy life, turn around, pick up that child, and hold her in my arms. Because it was not going to go away, and because I knew that part of me deserved my attention, I decided it was time to give full attention to my grief.

That Saturday morning I took the phone off the hook, put on a fresh pot of Starbucks, and pulled out five shoe boxes full of family photos. I'd purchased brand new Creative Memory albums and colorful stickers and had decided to make a picture album of the last ten years of our life as a family. I would walk through each year and celebrate the genuine love and joy we'd had. When I was finished I wanted to give it to my stepson, Mike, as a tangible memory that I especially had loved him and that his father and I had loved each other.

I spent the day arranging the pictures in chronological order and grouping them by events or holidays. First was Mike and me on the elephant ride at the Indio Date Festival, his little two-year-old legs spread straight out over the elephant's back while he waved at the camera. On another page was his first slumber party, when Dad brought home his fireman gear and let all the boys try it on. Photographs captured the whipped cream fights on his eighth birthday, Disneyland, Fisherman's Wharf in San Francisco, and riding on the ski boat in Lake Tahoe. I found funny photos of him dressed up in costumes and tender pictures of him in bed asleep with his cousin, Joe. I was reminded of the year my husband and I stayed up late nights in the garage, making stilts for all the kids for Christmas. Others pictured Boy Scout award dinners, Mike's first communion, and the birthday we gave him his first pocketknife. I bawled my eyes out when I tenderly pasted the photos of our anniversary party and our vacation right before my ex-husband left. There we all are, arms around each other. I know that real love and hidden problems between adults *can* coexist. The camera doesn't lie.

I spent that weekend and the next few days alternating between laughing out loud and weeping silently. No holding back, I let deep, mournful, gushing tears flow. I honored my grief without guilt or regret.

A week later I finished the album, one family's life and my dreams preserved between plastic pages. I invited my ex and stepson over to pick it up. Having made colored copies for myself, I then presented the album to my stepson. We all cried and had one last "family" hug. It was an affirming, cleansing ritual of release for me.

Grief Is God's Gift

Everyone's grief is unique, but everyone's grief is the same. The entire grieving process is marked by a vague outline of five general stages: shock/denial, anger, bargaining, depression, and acceptance. For each of us, however, the order in which we go through the stages and the timing and intensity vary. Feelings (sometimes specific, sometimes vague) can come and go and come again when we least expect them.

The stage of grieving when we weep and wail over our losses can be called bereavement or mourning. When I made the photo album, I was in deep bereavement, mourning the loss of all that I'd held dear. It was a necessary path of healing which my emotions automatically would have taken if I had not tried to shove them down. We know God created a system of healing in our physical bodies. Why do we forget he also created a system of healing for our minds and emotions as well? Mourning is a self-limiting, emotional cleansing, and healing process.

Some Thoughts about Grief

- Grief is agonizing. Grief is overpowering. Grief is *normal.*
- Grief can sneak up and overtake us unless we turn to face it and embrace it. To get beyond grief we must go through it, not around it.
- We can't do our grief work in isolation. To heal, we need to have someone who will listen. Helen Keller said, "When it seems our sorrow is too great to be borne, let us think of the great family of the heavy-hearted into which our grief has given us entrance, and inevitably, we will feel about us their arms, their sympathy, their understanding."
- Grief is like pulling out an infected splinter. We keep putting it off, because we know the pain we'll feel when we have to dig it out. We forget that afterward the constant soreness of the wound will end.

- Grief comes in waves. Some waves are bigger than others, but if we learn how to release them in healthy ways, the waves will get smaller over time.
- Grief's duration and intensity is not necessarily tied to the number of years we were married. Some people with shorter marriages will experience deeper grieving than others.
- The grieving process for second and third marriages can be more intense because of the extra feelings of failure and diminished hope for future success.
- The grieving process for second and third marriages also can be shorter because the individual has learned from previous experience how to more quickly accept reality, express emotions, and release the past.
- Grief can be interrupted by other tragedies and may have to be resumed in the future.

Unhealthy Grieving

Signs of abnormal grieving include enshrinement, which, to some degree, keeps us stuck in denial. Although he may have moved out years ago, some women keep their husband's pictures on the walls, in conversation refer to him as if they were still married, and harbor a futile hope that he will return. They never will move from their pain or be healed until they face facts and release the grief.

Lingering in depression longer than we need to is another form of unhealthy grieving. Mourning periods will vary for divorced women, but if we allow all our feelings to surface, take steps to process and release them, we should not grieve deeply for much longer than a year or two. This is only a general guideline; depending on the length and intensity of the marriage and the emotional maturity of the individual, this period could be a little shorter or longer. If you find yourself immobilized, or if your depression adversely affects your relationships for much longer, please get professional counseling to help you complete the process.

Well-meaning people, especially those who are uncomfortable with your situation and can't accept where you are in your grieving process, may say things like, "Snap out of it!" . . . "Just ignore those feelings and they eventually will go away" . . . "Stop talking about it; you're just bringing up all the misery again" . . . or "Bury yourself at work or in the kids; that will help you get over it more quickly."

Sometimes those unhealthy directives are self-induced, running in our heads like old cassette tapes from our parents, teachers, or other social influences from our childhood or the past.

Because of our tender mother's hearts, probably the bit of bad advice hardest to ignore is, "The kids need you now. You have to forget yourself and be there for *them*!" ARGHHH! That's the worst thing you can do*!* Moms need to be well on the way to health and emotional wholeness before they can help their children.

Imagine you've all been in a terrible car accident. In the deafening silence that follows the crash you start to hear your children's cries in the rubble. You know you must get to them! We all know we'd walk through fire or step on glass, and wouldn't feel a thing, until we got to our children. But if our thigh was sliced open and our artery was spurting out blood, we'd have the sense to know our own lives were being threatened and that we'd be no help at all to our kids if we are dead. So we stop just a moment, rip off our leather purse handle, and tie a makeshift tourniquet around our leg to stop the bleeding. Then we run like the devil to our babies.

Some emotional wounds from divorce can be tolerable (like the fire and glass) and we can minister to our children while we ourselves are in pain. Remember, though, some wounds are so devastating that unless we put ourselves first and get the healing we need, we will be emotionally dead and unable to run to or help our children.

In fact, the longer we delay our own emotional healing, the greater the odds of our children suffering permanent emotional damage because of our inability to be there for them.

Getting through Grief

Receive the Truth. Admit the reality of all aspects of your situation. Say it out loud and talk about it as much or as often as you need with a trusted friend, family member, or support group. Talk about it openly with the kids so you can teach them a healthy mourning process. Write down your losses on paper.

Recall the Loss. Talking about it is only the first step. Too often we stay stuck at the cognitive level of reality, trying to keep our emotions under control. This is when revisiting the past can play a part in the healing process.

Let yourself remember, imagine, look at old photos, play the old music, pack up the old things, and recall warm memories. Cry, get mad, and then cry again. Keep a box of Kleenex and a cold washcloth handy when you do this! Tell yourself it's okay and part of the process of moving on.

You know how wound up the kids get in the car after a few hours? If you just kept driving and screaming at them to be still every few minutes, you'd keep screaming louder and more frequently. Eventually you might become so distracted you'd drive into oncoming traffic and kill everyone. Emotions are like our kids in the car. Wise moms always know when to stop, let them get out to eat, run hard, and play. After they've been released in a controlled, safe environment, they will crawl back in the car and fall asleep while you continue to cruise contentedly through life.

Release the Past. Make sure you've allowed yourself sufficient time for crying or getting out your emotions. When you think you are ready, ritual is a good way of releasing. These women took the following empowering and healing steps:

> "I sat down and went through the whole wedding album and then packed it up and put it away for my children when they get married." —*Nancy*

"I took all the towels and sheets we'd picked out together, recalling the fun times we'd had outfitting out home, and gave them to Goodwill. It felt good to remember but also good to get rid of the reminders." —*Tricia*

"I took all his pictures down off the walls, but I let the kids put them up in their rooms. It was a small step, but it had a big healing effect on me." —*Barbara*

"I gave my wedding ring stone back to my mother-in-law because it had been hers. Then I had the gold and other diamonds made into a ring for my daughter." —*Suzanne*

"I started going to another grocery store so I wouldn't keep torturing myself with memories. I was surprised how that little change helped me let go of the past." —*Cindy*

Reinvest Yourself. Mourning requires large amounts of physical, mental, emotional, and spiritual energy. (Too bad we can't lose weight from all the energy we expend in grieving!) When you've *received the truth, recalled the loss, and released the past,* you will have much more time and energy to spend with God and yourself, your family, your friends, and community.

What to Look For

After healthy mourning, you'll begin to see the difference between tears of sorrow and tears of hopelessness. A good sign that you are healing well is that you're able to talk about the past, see old photos, or hear an old song without crying, getting angry, or becoming bitter. When that happens, celebrate the Master's healing touch. Because wounds leave scars, your divorce always will have some residual effect. Don't worry. Scars don't hurt, and they are reminders of the good work that your Heavenly Father can and will do for you through this sorrow.

What Does My Fear Say?

I don't want to grieve any more. It's too big. It's too painful. I'm sick of it. I want to move on. It doesn't feel good. What will people think if I am weak with grief? Why can't I just avoid it? I'll be fine, really I will, won't I?

What Does My Faith Say?

I know God has given me tears for a reason. He designed me to grieve so that I could heal. I will not be afraid of the pain, knowing he will give me his grace to get through it. After all, God's people wept. Jesus wept. I am not alone.

Love Letter

LITTLE ONE,

Hear my voice. Let me rock you gently and calm your soul. Clear your mind of all worry and anxiety and listen for my words of love, my promise of hope.

Your Loving Father

❧ 13 ❧

Choosing Faith Over Fear

Wishing to encourage her young son's progress on the piano, a mother took her boy to a Paderewski concert. After they were seated, the mother spotted an old friend in the audience and walked down the aisle to greet her. Seizing the opportunity to explore the wonders of the concert hall, the little boy rose and eventually explored his way through a door marked No Admittance. When the house lights dimmed and the concert was about to begin, the mother returned to her seat and discovered her child was missing. Suddenly, the curtains parted and spotlights shone on the impressive Steinway on stage. In horror, the mother saw her little boy was seated at the keyboard, innocently picking out "Twinkle, Twinkle, Little Star". At that moment, the great piano master made his entrance, quickly moved to the piano, and whispered in the startled boy's ear, "Don't quit. Keep playing." More than a little nervous, the boy obediently kept on.

Then, leaning over, Paderewski reached down with his left hand and began filling in a bass part. Soon his right arm reached around to the other side of the child and he added a running obligato. Together the old master and the young novice transformed a frightening situation into a wonderfully creative experience.

The audience was so mesmerized that they couldn't recall what else the great master played, only the classic, "Twinkle, Twinkle Little Star."

That's the way it is with God. What we can accomplish on our own is hardly noteworthy. We try our best, but the results aren't exactly graceful concertos. However, with the hand of the Master, even our most feeble attempts can be made truly beautiful. *(Author unknown)*

This short story illustrates several principles, but one that particularly fits the problem of divorce is *learning to choose faith over fear*. In this touching tale we are told how everyone is feeling: the mother is aghast, the piano master is delighted, and the boy is frightened by the lights and the sea of faces, and at the prospect of getting in trouble.

Despite his fears, however, the young boy decides to trust. Maybe something in the older man's voice calmed him. Whatever the reason, the boy chose *faith over fear*, and look what happened!

The Courtroom in Our Heads

Sometimes we might be like that little boy. We're scared, but we can choose to trust anyway. Having faith doesn't mean you aren't afraid. Having faith means that you can act despite your fears. You could say faith is what you *know* in your head, fear is what you might *feel* in your heart. For example, I know I am not really still hungry and that extra chocolate doughnut will be bad for me, but I feel like I really, really need it!

We most often get into trouble when *what we know* conflicts with *what we feel*. (I *know* I should be kind to my neighbor, but some days I just don't *feel* like it.)

God did not leave us without tools to choose faith over fear. Whenever we choose to hold an attitude or execute some action, we can rely on our mind, emotions, conscience, intuition, and will.

To better understand how all these work together, or clash, consider the following hypothetical story (in jest, of course):

The thought has just entered your mind to kill your ex-husband who, for the fifth month in a row, has failed to send the child support check.

Enter the black-robed judge, your WILL, who will make the final decision to kill or not to kill.

The first attorney is your MIND, which presents to the court facts: everything you have learned, been taught, read, absorbed, and intellectually accumulated. Some information is true and, unfortunately, some is false. This guy is cool, calm, and collected.

The next attorney is your EMOTIONS. She'll present your feelings of fear, hope, anger, love, lust, as well as your dreams, desires, and rationalizations. She's deep, passionate, and powerful.

The court's advocate is your SPIRIT, which has the direct information link to God (like the red phone to the Russian Commissar) and includes your conscience and intuition. The SPIRIT almost glows from within and sits at the left hand of the judge's bench.

Once the thought of murder enters your mind, the arguments begin.

The EMOTIONS scream, "Kill!" The Spock-like MIND interrupts, very calmly of course, and says, "If you kill, you will go to jail and never see your kids or the light of day again."

The WILL listens to both sides and then consults the SPIRIT. "What have *you* to say?" the judge inquires.

The SPIRIT says, "God will make all things right in the end. He says let go and learn to love your ex-husband. It's right here in the ordinance (his Word) and in your conscience."

"Learn to love him?" screeches the EMOTIONS? "Arghh-h-h-h!!"

The MIND nods in agreement. "Yes, I daresay I agree with the SPIRIT. It makes sense to me. In checking my files I see that God has taken care of you in the past and the statistical data proves he will again in the future."

"But he doesn't pay the child support and we're starving!" cries the EMOTIONS.

"We know," says the MIND, "But you are remembering injustices all the way back from your childhood, and you don't trust *anyone* to take care of you. It's time to listen to us. Our information says everything will be okay."

"Yes," says the SPIRIT. "God has given you his Word to prove it."

The EMOTIONS sit down while the MIND and SPIRIT come over and pat her on the back. "Your Honor?" they inquire.

"After careful consideration of the facts and feelings, tempered by your Spirit's faith, I have made my decision. Of course there will be no murder this time."

BANG goes the gavel.

What We Can Do

It's pretty funny when you think of it, because it's a rather realistic drama of what goes on with us all day long. That courtroom scene can happen in a split second every time we are tempted to sin. That's why it's so important to make sure we:

- Keep our MIND educated with the right information, such as God's Word and other reliable sources. Otherwise we'll base decisions on lies.
- Develop a good conscience and constantly stay in touch with the SPIRIT who dwells in us and lets us hear God's voice. Some people listen to the human mind and emotions, but never consult their spiritual side.
- Work through counseling to heal damaged EMOTIONS, because when they are out of control they can take over. Sometimes you can trust emotions and sometimes you can't. Emotions are fickle and fleeting and always need to be weighed with other information.

- When our *mind, emotions, and conscience* are working together, the *will* (who calls the final shot) will have a much easier job.

$\mathcal{A}$ Bad Rap for Emotions

Ever have a child who threw a major tantrum? When our emotions are damaged from any kind of past abuse, they will be like that child, crying out for what they want and trying every trick in the book to get it, whether it's good for them or not. If we haven't learned to calm ourselves emotionally and function on facts and our God-given authority over sin, we will not be able to parent ourselves very well, and our emotions will run amok. Just as a mother can calm her child's tantrum, so the mind and spirit can keep us in balance.

Let's not forget, though, that emotions can be good. God-given emotions help us love, trust, enjoy, value, treasure, and appreciate. It's only when they are damaged that they become negative. The problem is not really our emotions; it's that we too often let our emotions stay in control, instead of tempering them with what we know and what God tells us through his Word and others.

Our emotions can win for a better good, as long as they lead us to the right decision and we are listening to and in tune with the Spirit. Here's an example:

Let's say your ex-husband just called and asked for the children for the Thanksgiving holiday. You normally alternate holidays with him and this is not his year. Beside, you were planning a trip to your mother's so the kids could see their cousins. He's been depressed lately and his girlfriend just left him. Intellectually you realize you owe him no favors, because he gets plenty of visitation time. You also know he will have the children for half of the Christmas vacation and next year he'll get all of Thanksgiving. You make your mental checklist of all the reasons why you should just kindly tell him you already have plans and maybe offer to let him have them Wednesday night before you leave. A gentle tugging at your heart stops your thought process and a sweet, soft voice inside you says, "He's their father. He's doing the best he can, and he is lonely." Your empathetic emotions are joined in by your spirit, which reminds you that whatsoever you do for the least of these, you do for Jesus (Matt. 25:40). You check your emotions to see if any manipulation is going on, or if any guilt is behind the voice, and you recognize only the clarity of true compassion. So, without any intellectual reason for your choice, you pick up the phone to let him know the kids are his for the holiday, no strings attached. Well done!

Healing Emotions from Divorce

When a doctor first examines you and wants to prescribe the right treatment for your injury or illness, he first must hear about and understand your pain. He needs to know where it hurts, how long the pain has been going on, and how it started. That's what we've done with the first section of this book. We've listed the areas of pain that result from divorce and described some of the symptoms. Understanding the source of the pain is the first step in understanding what course of action must be taken for your cure.

The next section of the book is like the talk the doctor gives you when he comes back into the room after your initial examination. In his hands he's got a few x-rays and maybe the results of a blood test. He invites you to view the screen as he points out broken bones or bruised organs and explains how and why they need to function. He may warn you about what will happen if changes aren't made or problems aren't fixed. He's sharing the medical principles upon which your treatment will be based. After that he'll instruct you to establish new priorities in your health care and give you a written sheet of new practices to maintain your health.

You've already learned the first step in the healing process: to start developing all of our attitudes and making all of our decisions based on what we know (our faith) instead of what we feel (our fear). Are you ready to move on?

*W*hat Does My Fear Say?

My fear is all over the place. It's in my anger, hurt, depression, and loneliness. I feel overwhelmed and unable to move sometimes. This process is going to take forever, and I'm sick of it already!

*W*hat Does My Faith Say?

If the only thing I ever do is start to recognize the difference between my fear and my faith, I will be okay. Faith is a gift. I can ask for it in all circumstances, and he will give it. Like the boy and the piano master, he and I can make beautiful music together.

SECTION

II

Examining the Principles

Love Letter

MY SWEET DAUGHTER,

I know you are frustrated. Sometimes the pain you suffer seems to make no sense at all. Do you know that through the hardships you have had to endure I am trying to prepare you for and protect you from even worse problems? Will you learn to relax and trust me?

Your Loving Father

❧ 14 ❧

Understanding the "Why?"

One early Saturday morning in 1962, my little brother Charlie, my sister Barb, and I threw on our jeans, wolfed down some Rice Krispies, and hopped on our Schwinn bicycles. We rode down the street, past the cemetery, and up into the almond orchard where our neighbor, Mr. Parker, was getting ready to harvest almonds. The orchard was our playground. In spring, when the trees were like cotton candy with pink and white blossoms, we girls would play house and help the boys dig underground forts. Every summer one of my brothers accidentally set the orchard on fire after sneaking Mom's cigarettes, but the fire department always came to the rescue before any real damage was done. On this crisp, fall morning, the trees were green and full of fruit.

Mr. Parker was a quiet man, with big biceps, a Navy tattoo, and an old Chevy pickup truck. We watched as he unrolled and shook out a large tarp and laid it down under one slender almond tree whose branches hung heavy with nuts. Then, much to my horror and surprise, Mr. Parker pulled out the biggest sledgehammer I think I have ever seen, told us to step back, and gave the tree a mighty whack!

The poor tree shook from top to bottom and in an instant it was raining almonds, every branch giving up its fruit. The noise of the hard-shelled nuts hitting the tarp stopped as suddenly as it had started. We all stood there silent and wide-eyed. "Well, whadaya waiting fer?"

Mr. Parker said, as he threw us each a gunnysack. As we scrambled on all fours to gather up the almonds, I crawled close to see where Mr. Parker had whacked the tree. I found no visible sign of damage to the trunk, and the tree stood tall and apparently unharmed.

Little did I know that this Saturday morning event would, years later, teach me a spiritual lesson: God often uses the hard whacks of life to teach us to let go. When we do, we can look back and see that it was necessary to give up what we were holding onto so tightly. In his loving care, he ensures that when it's all over, we're still standing and ready to grow into the next season of our life.

When I was married, I worked hard to help pay the mortgage on our beautiful home with the large open kitchen and a yard lush with fruit trees. I loved to set a pretty table, and regularly hosted dinners, parties, and teas. I also could afford car payments, piano lessons, fun Christmases, vacations, and shopping. When I was forced to let go of all that in my divorce, I was like that almond tree. I see now that I had held on to things a little too tightly . . . until I learned that *the best things in life aren't things*. Through the pain, God freed my grasp of all those "almonds" so that I could more easily reach out and hold his hand.

God Wants Us to Release Our Grip

More than half of the women who come into our DivorceCare meetings ask, "Why did God allow this divorce to happen?" In his book *When God Doesn't Make Sense*, Dr. James Dobson provides some very clear and compassionate reasons why God would allow bad things to happen to good people. But we never will understand everything during this lifetime, and that's best. As Dr. Dobson says, "There is nothing God wants of us more than the exercise of our faith"[1]

Walking in faith instead of fear (the basis of all painful emotions) is tough. If you're like me you want answers! Yet, in my life I have seen why God might allow tragedy, failure, and pain to befall us. One reason is to help us let go of the things to which we hold on too tightly.

God Wants to Build Character in Us

Gary Richmond, minister to single parents at First Evangelical Free Church in Fullerton, California, shares a delightful story in his book *It's a Jungle Out There*. Gary, who was a veterinary assistant at the Los Angeles Zoo, tells about the birth of a baby giraffe.

When Gary arrived at the giraffe barn, he noticed right away that the mother giraffe was giving birth standing up, her hindquarters nearly ten feet off the ground. The calf's front hooves and head were already out and Gary, worried that the baby would be hurt falling from such a height, asked if they should go in and help. The vet warned him to stand back because the mother had enough strength in her legs to kick Gary's head off, and that's just what she'd do if anyone approached her baby.

Minutes later the baby hurled forth, falling ten feet and landing on his back. Within seconds he rolled upright with his legs tucked under his body. The mother took a quick look, positioned herself directly over her baby, and then did something that shocked Gary.

She swung her leg out and kicked her baby so hard it sent him sprawling head over heels. The baby didn't get up. Mom positioned herself over baby again and kicked it again, repeating the violent process as the baby struggled each time to rise. Mom never gave up until, amidst cheers from the zoo staff, the baby stood for the first time...wobbly and shaking, but on its own.

Gary writes, "She wants it to remember how it got up...that's why she knocked it down. In the wild it would need to get up as soon as possible to follow the herd and avoid being eaten alive by lions, hyenas, or leopards." He adds, "I've learned that when a trial comes along, it is God helping me remember how it was that I got up before. He is urging me to always walk with him—in his shadow under his care."[2]

God has a lot to teach us through the hard kicks of divorce. We can grow stronger, run faster, and maybe learn to be smart enough to stay out of the jungle next time! We can learn to:

Become less self-centered
Become more compassionate
Love more
Forgive
Put others first
Get our priorities back on track
Find peace in all circumstances

God Wants to Bring Greater Good from Our Pain

The story goes that the only survivor of a shipwreck was washed up on a small uninhabited island. Day and night he prayed feverishly for God to rescue him, and every day he scanned the horizon for help, but none came. Exhausted, he managed to build a small hut out of driftwood to protect him from the elements and to store his few possessions.

One day, after scavenging for food, he arrived home to find his little hut in flames, the smoke rolling up to the sky. The worst had happened; everything was lost. He was stunned with grief and anger. "God, how could you do this to me!" he cried. He slept among the burning embers and wept at the long days of rebuilding he feared were ahead.

Early the next day, however, he awakened to the sound of a ship coming to the island. It had come to rescue him. "How did you know I was here?" the weary man asked of his rescuers.

"We saw your smoke signal," they replied.

Even though divorce seems like it destroyed all we had, it can be the method through which God rescues us from a life of apathy toward him, an immature faith, or a wordly focus.

Through the burning down of our lives, we can be rescued from ourselves. We can begin to look at and work on character defects we may have ignored. Even though we might get depressed thinking of the rebuilding ahead, we can reach greater levels of maturity and become better women, mothers, and friends. If we ever remarry, the lessons we learn from divorce also can make us better wives.

Early in my last marriage, we began to have trouble, so taking direction from our counselor I worked hard at learning to let go of unrealistic expectations, first about my husband, and then about other people. I also learned to be more patient with my husband and with others whose temperaments differed from mine. I eliminated the clutter in my schedule and made time for quiet. I learned to listen more and talk less. I worked hard at becoming a much more balanced person in all areas of my life. It was hard, but it was worth it.

Part of my difficulty in accepting my husband's choice to end the marriage was that I thought we'd learned so much and made so many improvements. Yet we can live with and love others and never really see or know the agonizing emotional turmoil they are experiencing. My husband had been terribly abused as a child and struggled privately with the consequences, so no matter how much we loved each other, I could not help him. I had to accept being powerless. For a strong woman, that's scary.

After grieving my divorce, and accepting my financial losses, I realized I still had more to learn about trusting God. I started getting anxious about my future and worried that no one ever would love me again. Thankfully, I had learned to fall back on principles whenever my emotions start to rise and knew I had to go right back to my Heavenly Father for leadership. "What do *you* say about my future?" I asked him. I already knew the answer. He's told me over and over every time I read Jeremiah 29:11. He knows the plans he has for me, plans for my welfare, not for woe. He has great things in store for my future, and for the first time in my life I really, truly believed that with all my heart and soul. Through my divorce God brought me closer to him. And that's the greatest rescue of all.

God Can Use Divorce to Show Forth His Glory

Since I like happy endings, I absolutely love the story of sisters Martha and Mary and their brother, Lazarus. In John 11:17–44 we read that Lazarus was dying and, knowing Jesus had been healing all types of diseases, they sent word for him to come immediately. But he didn't. Lazarus died, was buried, and lay in his tomb for three days before Jesus showed up. Mary was livid.

I can almost hear the bitterness in her voice when she reminded Jesus that he had not been there for her. After all, they were dear friends! She and her family had been good and did not deserve this tragedy. Many of us divorced women might feel the same way. Why? Why? Why?

"Lord, if you had been here, my brother would not have died," Mary said in verse 32.

Notice, however, that Martha never cut off Jesus completely. She vented her emotions I'm sure, but she immediately expressed her faith by saying, "But I know that even now God will give you whatever you ask" (John 11:22).

Most of us divorced women can come to (or are already at) that place of faith where we believe that God will restore our homes, our cars, our bank accounts, our lifestyle, or other things we lost in the divorce. But, like Mary, our focus is still on what we lost. God calls us to look beyond that.

Jesus was still trying to make that point to Martha. When he told her that her brother would rise from the dead, she may have given her answer rather flippantly, something like "Yeah, yeah I know. We'll *all* rise on the last day at the resurrection. Duh!"

I think Jesus then might have put his hands on her shoulders and his face right in hers, nose to nose, eyes locked, intense, and maybe frustrated, and said to her whom he loved, "I AM the resurrection and the life! Me, Martha! Look at me! What have I been telling you all these years? Open your eyes!"

Jesus desperately wanted her to look past her earthly desires and to see the bigger glory that was being shown. He wanted her to see the Father's magnificence, power, and glory. He wants that for us as well.

Are we still focused on what we lost, what we need, what we're hoping God will restore to us? Are we still demanding answers or have we opened our eyes to see only him, pure God, pure love, in all his splendor, power, and glory?

What Does My Fear Say?

I am scared that I will continue to be knocked around in life, suffering over and over, or that I will be exhausted from fighting the world . . . and for what? It seems so pointless at times.

What Does My Faith Say?

I may not understand everything, but I know I can trust God. I will start to see all my problems as ways he can develop me into the woman he wants. In each difficulty in my life I'll look for the character quality I lack, and, with his grace, I will work on becoming more beautiful than ever.

Love Letter

PRECIOUS ONE,

I will keep telling you how much I love you as long as you need to hear it. Even when you don't feel like trusting me, I will be there for you always, until the end of time. Just for today, just for right now trust in me and I will deliver you. Trust in me and you will not be disappointed.

Your Loving Father

❧ 15 ❧

Learning to Trust

id you ever stop to think that God could teach us
important spiritual truths through email? Every
day in my computer mailbox I have to delete all kinds of junk:
chain letters, credit card offers, and cyber-myths, such as the infa-
mous $250 recipe for Nieman Marcus cookies! But this story has
come across my screen several times, and never fails to inspire me
to trust God:

The Pearls

Little Rachel was a cheery five-year-old who loved to go shopping
with her mother. Mother always let her visit the toy aisles, where
she'd drool over the glittery plastic high heels, sparkling tiaras, and
plastic bead jewelry. One day she saw the most beautiful white
pearl necklace in a shiny foil box. They looked almost real!

"Oh Mommy! Can I have them? Please, please, *please?*

Mother checked the price tag and wisely told Rachel, "Honey,
these are $2.95 plus tax. You only have a dollar of your chore
money left at home. But if you want to do some extra work

around the house to earn the rest of the money, I will get them for you today. Deal?"

When they got home, Rachel ran to her Barbie bank and shook out four quarters and a dime. Then she put on her new pearl necklace. "Mom, here's my money. Tonight I'll ask Daddy if I can do anything for him. Thanks!" and Rachel gave her mom a big hug.

Rachel loved her pearls. That night she showed the necklace to Daddy when he read her a bedtime story. "They're lovely, sweetie," said Dad. "You look like a princess!"

One night after Daddy finished their usual bedtime story, he asked his daughter, "Rachel, do you love me?"

"*Yes*, Daddy! You know I do."

"Then may I please have your pearls?"

"My pearls?" Rachel looked a little dismayed. "Well, you can have my plastic tiara. You know the one I got from Grandma last year. It's really pretty."

"No, honey," Dad said. " That's all right. Good night."

Every night when Daddy finished the bedtime story he asked her the same question. "Can I have your pearls?" And every night Rachel would instead offer him something else in her treasured collection of stuffed toys or dolls. She loved her pearls more than anything and hated to give them up.

After a while, though, Rachel could see the disappointment in her Daddy's face and she started to feel bad. Daddy was so wonderful and she was starting to get a funny feeling in her tummy whenever she said no to him. She realized that she loved him more than the pearls. Finally, one night Rachel waited for Daddy to ask.

"Yes! Daddy. You can have them!" and Rachel reached under her pillow and cheerfully handed the necklace to her father.

Daddy had a surprise of his own. He smiled, got up, went to his room, came back, and gave Rachel a black velvet case. It was gorgeous. She opened it up and inside was a small strand of real pearls, just like Mommy's. She threw her arms around her father's neck and hugged him tight.

God Has Pearls for Us

Are you like little Rachel? Are you clinging tightly to all the things you thought you wanted, wishing to get back what you lost, or fearing the loss of more in the future? We forget that our Heavenly Father is always waiting for us to give up our own desires so that he can replace them with something even better. We don't trust him.

Whenever we are hurt or disappointed by someone's action or failure to take action, we begin to lose trust. The more rejection or abuse we suffer, the less trust we have, and not just in the person who failed us, but in life in general.

We divorced women lose trust in our ex-husbands and often all men. We lose trust in marriage. We lose trust in the court system that fails to provide justice in custody, visitation, or child support issues. We lose trust that our children will not be turned against us by their father or new stepparent. Worst of all, we lose trust in ourselves and God.

Women Who Don't Trust

Here's what some divorced women have shared with me about trust:

Donna said, "I think I've worked through all my issues, but I just don't trust men. And, sadly, it's almost like I don't trust God, either. The last two relationships I've had (the only two since I've been divorced) were supposedly good Christian men. I was even more upset and disappointed when those relationships didn't work out. I felt used. Why would God allow me to be used over and over again?"

Like Donna, we may love God and know that he has power over our lives, but forget that he doesn't orchestrate every minute of our existence. God never deliberately sets others against us. He's given us all free will so sometimes others get to be in control.

Because human nature is sinful, we're going to get hurt. It's mythical thinking to expect constant protection from pain and problems. Pain and problems are tools God can use to mature us.

If Donna is like I was, she hasn't developed a clear insight into human behavior and/or doesn't know how to set healthy boundaries. As a result, she gets used. Usually we fail to see red flags early in relationships because of our own lack of education and because we don't *want* to. We also fail to set boundaries for ourselves because we do not know how and we do not love, value, and take care of ourselves as God does.

Whether we are married or divorced, it's never too late to educate ourselves and learn ways to prevent people from hurting or using us. In relationships, we have both rights (to fair treatment) *and* responsibilities (to not remain victims).

Of course at times we all will get hurt again, no matter what we do. That's life! God says, "You can't always do it on your own, sweetheart . . . I keep trying to tell you—come to *me*."

Rene told me of her lack of trust: "I am only now learning to trust again. I've met someone wonderful, but the thought of marrying again and possibly having him cheat on me scares me to death. With God's help I hope to work through this."

Sadly, many women talk about God's help but do nothing to help themselves. When we discover we have cancer, we pray for God's help but we also go see a doctor. In healing from divorce, God's help most often comes through human means: godly doctors, counselors, mentors, teachers, pastors, books, tapes, videos, radio broadcasts, and more. God wants us to trust him and to take responsibility.

I think God probably wants Rene to learn which mental and emotional patterns are affecting her choices and decisions, and get them back in tune with his way. Also, as she lets what she *knows* take charge, then what she *feels* will calm down. Like Rene, sometimes we know we can trust God, we just don't feel like we can.

Gina writes, "The biggest scare from my divorce is my inability to trust. I have a real problem with that. But I think that's also due to the fact I never trusted my family. When I went through my divorce, my family alienated me because they didn't know how to deal with it. They were in denial about the whole thing. My mother said, 'Oh, all men cheat on their wives.' "

Gina's not alone. The lack of trust reaches beyond a failed marriage partner to our family, friends, and anyone in the world who has ever hurt or abandoned us in any way. Lack of trust is simply a fear of future pain or loss, and a lack of faith that we can do anything about it.

Genuine Trust, False Trust

Some of us, myself included, will trust people simply because we *want* to and because it's easier than always being on guard. We place false trust in the other person based solely on our emotions and not on reality. Developing genuine trust in another person requires self-restraint and work. When we give unearned and untested trust, we foolishly set ourselves up to be hurt.

Genuine trust develops when we take responsibility for loving ourselves enough to establish reasonable physical, mental, and emotional protection, and when we hold the other person accountable to our boundaries.

Withholding Trust

Sometimes we purposely withhold trust, even when someone has made efforts to rebuild it. People may be tap dancing as fast as they can to regain our faith and confidence in them, but we refuse to give it. Why? We might be holding onto the power we feel when we know they want our trust; withholding it keeps us in the driver's seat. Sometimes we withhold trust because we want to keep pointing the finger at these people, reminding the world that they failed and we were the victims. Are you withholding trust out of a vengeful spirit? Are you refusing to trust again because you like being the victim?

To cure the lack of faith that's behind any of our trust issues, we can do the following:

Give Yourself Permission Not To Trust People. I'm not talking about withholding trust out of bitter cynicism. Whether we love or hate them, sometimes we just can't trust people. Trust can come and go, be violated, and be rebuilt. Have you ever had a friend or loved one who was always late for everything? Obviously you couldn't trust this person to be on time, but did you complain about it all the time or do something about it? With my habitually late girlfriend, I automatically add thirty minutes to any schedule we set. Since I can't change her, I change my attitude and my actions. I love her, but I still can't trust her in this area.

At a DivorceCare meeting, Mattie shared that her greatest enlightenment during the twelve-week course was that she could forgive her ex-husband, be more gracious with him, but still not have to trust him. "I thought when you were loving or kind toward someone you had to trust them, too. I thought that not trusting someone was an insult to them. I see now that a lack of trust sometimes is simply recognizing another's limitations."

Set and Enforce Healthy Boundaries. Nancy's ex-husband Jim, is always late picking up their son, Trevor, for weekends. Typically Jim calls up and says he will not be there for another hour. Rather than letting this affect her plans to meet friends in thirty minutes, she can leave Trevor with a neighbor or relative or take him with her. Nancy shared, "I don't have to wait at home, miss the movie, or point my finger in anger and say, 'You #$%@&! I can't trust you.' I've learned to put the responsibility back where it belongs and to take care of myself instead of expecting others to always do it exactly the right way or my way. I can't control that, but I can control which option I choose. That way, I don't get angry."

Allow Time for Rebuilding. Once you start setting healthy boundaries, people are much more likely to begin to change their behavior, but some never will. If you are in a relationship and are just starting to set new boundaries, give the other person time to respond with new behaviors of his or her own. Rebuilding trust takes time.

Trust God. Just like the dollar bill says, "In God we trust". Some people we never will be able to trust. Even people we *do* trust will sometimes let us down. At times I can't even trust myself! But we can always trust God.

What Does My Fear Say?

I don't trust anyone. I've been hurt, lied to, cheated on, and disappointed so many times I don't know how I can ever trust again. It would be stupid to trust again and let myself be hurt. I refuse to let go of my fear and anger because I feel safer, somehow more in control, that way.

What Does My Faith Say?

When I refuse to trust it's because I am trying to do it all on my own . . . and I don't know how. I will start to develop healthy boundaries so I won't be victimized as much. I will accept that some people can't be trusted but I will not become bitter about it. I also will accept that I can't protect myself perfectly, and that's okay. Risk is part of getting the reward. I will let go of my fear, anger, and bitterness and give them to God . . . so he can give me real pearls of courage, confidence, wisdom, faith, and trust.

Love Letter

MY DAUGHTER,

There is a time for everything, and I have set the time for you. If you are open to my leading, I will make you more beautiful than you can imagine . . . in my time.

Your Loving Father

❧ 16 ❧

Giving It Time

Well-meaning friends commonly advise us—and we may even try to assure ourselves—that "Time heals all wounds." Wrong! Time alone does *not* heal all wounds. Let me share my sister Barb's story:

Barb and her boyfriend, Art, were in their second year of junior college and had been dating for some time. Art had proposed to Barb and given her a diamond engagement ring, but in the weeks that followed, normal prenuptial tension erupted into a fight, and Barb threw the ring at Art and stormed away. Art, wounded and nursing a broken heart, moved one hundred miles away to work in his father's store. Over the next few months, Barb began to miss Art terribly and, after a few hours of tossing and turning one night, she decided to do something about it. A little after midnight Barb, still living at home, got dressed, took the family car, and started driving through the night to Art. For almost the entire distance, the highway was flat, straight, and empty. Barb became drowsy and almost hypnotized by the passing yellow line. Finally nodding off, she veered off the road and crashed, landing upside down.

In a state of shock, Barb unfastened her seat belt and found her only way out was through the triangular window in the back seat. Squeezing herself through the small space, she climbed up the embankment and flagged down a passing Volkswagen Beetle. When the car pulled over, she begged the young teenagers inside, "Help me!"

The kids took one look at her and, without saying a word, sped away horrified. What was wrong? Later Barb learned that her face had been violently cut, and when she'd been hanging upside down the blood had gushed into her long, blonde hair. Once she was up and walking, the blood had then flowed downward and covered her head to toe. Also her nose had been severed and was hanging by a thin piece of skin. The kids in the car were terrified at the sight.

Within minutes, though, a big-rig truck driver who had witnessed the accident from about a mile back, pulled over and picked up Barb in his arms, lifted her up onto his seat, and raced her the three miles to the nearest hospital, in the town where Art lived. The driver later told Barb that he'd watched her car flip end-over-end five times before it landed in the gully.

Aware of the dangers of crash victims lapsing into shock, the trucker tried to keep Barb awake by talking to her and asking her to talk to him. When she didn't know what to say, Barb thought of a church song from her childhood that she sang until they reached the emergency room.

Immediately doctors rushed Barb into surgery, where they removed pieces of shattered glass, sewed her nose back on, and held her face together with more than one hundred stitches. The truck driver called Art who lived just a few blocks away. Art ran though the night in his bare feet, leaping over backyard fences to take the shortcut to the hospital to be with Barb.

Barb was okay, her face healed, she and Art got married, and the truck driver and his wife danced at their wedding. Yet, despite the happy ending, Barb still has a problem. A piece of windshield glass is still embedded in Barb's face, just below the bridge of her nose. The doctors decided not to cut deeper into her skin, so close to the eye, and hoped instead that it would work its way out eventually, like some glass shards will do. Barb's didn't. The glass has stayed in her face for more than twenty-five years, causing her irritation, redness, and difficulty wearing glasses. Rather than get the glass cut out, Barb has chosen to live with the problem.

How Our Divorce Is Like the Crash

Our divorces were traumatic like that car crash. We suffered emotional aches and pains, and some of us had blood running into our eyes for a long time. Maybe we reached out for help to friends, family, or the church and got nowhere. Maybe people took one look at us and ran the other way, politely cutting us out of social calendars and groups, or avoiding us altogether.

Like the truck driver, God saw the whole thing, and he's ready to pick us up and take us to the emergency room. We can trust him to always be there when we need him. But, like the truck driver, God usually delivers us into the hands of capable human doctors to take over and complete the healing process. Emotionally, we may want to climb up in the trucker's lap, sing sweet songs, and stay in the comfort of the cab. We're afraid of the doctors, nurses, and needles that come with full healing. While God wants us to feel his comfort, he also wants us to be willing to go through the hard, frightening, and painful process of emotional surgery.

That's what we've been doing in previous chapters by looking at our shock, anger, depression, guilt, grief, and fears. It's time to get those shards out of our lives so we can go on no longer emotionally crippled.

Nothing Changes if Nothing Changes

After the initial stitching up and other subsequent medical procedures, time healed some of Barb's wounds, but not all of them. Barb learned how to live with that remnant shard in her face, despite the fact it still causes her discomfort and slight disfigurement. One of the benefits and drawbacks of being creatures of habit is that over time we can get desensitized and numb to what hurts us.

Too many of us who get past the initial shock of divorce stop the healing process. We get back on our feet, regroup our finances, and, after a period, either start dating or nobly retreat into motherhood. We don't take the time or do the work to find out how we got there, what really happened, and what *in us* needs to be fixed.

Mental and emotional problems rarely work their way out automatically. They stay embedded and constantly cause trouble over the years. They infect our home life, our work, and our relationships with God and others. Some emotional problems even get worse over time. If we don't take steps, healing will not happen by itself.

How Long Does It Take to Heal from Divorce?

No one ever gets completely over a divorce, just as we never get over the death of a loved one. We always will have memories and always will have scars, but we can become healed enough to live full and fruitful lives.

Some psychologists say that the average divorce recovery time is at least one year for every year you were married. Most agree it takes a minimum of one year just to get over the shock and get back on your feet emotionally. Yet many people can stay stuck in denial for years.

If you were in a marriage that faltered hopelessly for years, or if you were in intensive counseling, you may already have done a lot of your grief work. By the time the divorce was filed you may have been well on your way to accepting reality and moving through the recovery process.

If you've been divorced before, you may move more quickly through the emotions this time, or it may take longer because of the added sense of multiple failures.

If you're young, you may be more optimistic than older women. Perhaps you did not lose as much, and your career is well established. You may assume there's still plenty of time to find Mr. Right and have children.

If you're in your thirties or forties, you may fear not being able to have more children, or any at all. It's also sometimes harder to get back into the workforce.

As for the hope of falling in love again and ever having a good marriage, divorced women in their fifties and sixties face bleak prospects. Most men their age are already married or in mid-life crisis and dating much younger women.

All these factors play into how long you will feel hurt, angry, or depressed. Temperaments also play a strong role, with some women eager to dig deep and take on the challenges of growth and recovery, and others naturally a little slower and more cautious. The extent of outside support (mentors, counselors, teachers) and the nature of our relationship to God also affects the time it takes to heal.

Each woman will move through her healing process at a different pace. The main focus of this time should be on:

- Not fooling ourselves that time will heal all
- Not hiding from deeper, emotional healing in religion, work, or mothering
- Not rushing through to get past the pain and to find only temporary peace
- Not replacing our relationship with God with relationships with others

The man at the pool in Bethesda waited for thirty years (John 5:1–18). The woman Jesus healed from bleeding had been sick for twelve years (Luke 8:43–48). Each also had to take an active part in the healing process: he had to get up and pick up his own mat, and she had to actively seek out help.

What steps will you now take toward healing? Don't let this period in your life be a waste of time.

*W*hat Does My Fear Say?

I'm afraid this is going to take forever! I hate that my feelings keep returning. When am I ever going to be my old self again? I just want to have fun, to have peace, to feel in control, and to return to life as it should be!

*W*hat Does My Faith Say?

If I really believe that God knows my needs and promises to meet them, and if I believe he will not make me suffer without reason, then I have nothing to fear. I will not focus on the length of time it takes to heal. I will use this time to become the woman he intended so that I can be fulfilled in his purpose. That will give me timeless joy, peace, and happiness.

Love Letter

DEAR ONE,

You may not want to change, but I desire it for you, and my grace will be sufficient for you. I will deliver you from your troubles, and you will remember who has saved you and brought you to maturity. You will honor me.

Your Loving Father

❧ 17 ❧

Growing in Grace

*G*race, according to Webster's, is: a divine influence renewing and morally strengthening man—or in our case, woman. When we ask for God's grace, we'd better be careful, because we're asking to *be changed.*

Change can be scary because we not only must leave our comfort zone, we might have to go out into a dark, unknown situation in which we feel powerless and out of control.

Who Moved My Cheese, a New York Times best-seller, is a delightful little allegory that says the road to happiness, fulfillment, and even life itself, is through . . . gulp . . . *change.* Two little mice, used to a comfortable spot in their maze, realize that their cheese is fast running out. To find a new food source, one mouse risks the unknown and ventures out into the scary dark maze. The other mouse, stuck stubbornly in denial, stays exactly where he's been all these years, and when the cheese is finally gone, he dies of hunger. The mouse who *changed* eventually finds a huge pile of the best cheese ever.

Divorce can be a wake-up call to make needed changes in our lives. When we begin to have true faith and trust in God, we can see our way out of lots of old habits and ways of thinking and into a different place where we might even find better cheese.

Change Means Getting Rid of Emotional Problems

I'm going to take you on an imaginary trip to the maternity ward. First, pick one of the emotional problems we suffer after divorce: anger, guilt, anxiety, fear, bitterness, or depression. Now imagine it inside you growing very slowly over time, as in the first trimester of pregnancy. Initially, you may not notice your emotional problem because the signs usually are small, but as time passes it just keeps growing, like a baby, eventually kicking and thrashing inside you.

As it gets larger, it begins to sap the bigger part of your food, vitamin, and mineral supply. If you have even been pregnant, you'll remember that your doctor quickly prescribed vitamins because your body was giving the first share of nutrients to your baby. You got tired faster, your teeth may have been robbed of calcium, and your body was depleted of essential nourishment. Emotional problems are the same. They take up the bigger share of your mental, emotional and spiritual energy, leaving you tired and prone to injury and poor health in all areas.

Remember the first day you just couldn't fit into your jeans anymore? Or maybe the day you bought your first maternity clothes or the day you started morning sickness was when you left the state of denial and finally accepted that someone else beside you was in you. With your emotional problems, however, you don't just work around it, changing your wardrobe. You call your doctor—it's time to give birth.

God, as your doctor, will help you through the hard labor of getting rid of your anger, anxiety, or fear, but he will not do it all for you. You have to push and breathe and keep on pushing and working through your emotional issues. Yes, it will hurt and take some time, but it will not kill you. He's there, but you have to do *your part* too. Then, right after delivery, he will take that problem. He wants you to let go so you can move on.

The funny thing is that your problem, although separate from you, is a part of you and you know the sound of its voice. After successfully working through your problem and giving it to God, you may long to run into the nursery and pick it up when you hear its lusty cry. You may want to hold onto and nurse your problem. It is hard to let go!

After You Work Through Problems

After you're delivered of a problem, you need to keep making changes in your life to reach full health. After divorce, you need to exercise, eat right, and get back into shape not only physically but also mentally, emotionally, and spiritually. That means changing your old habits and giving it time. Remember: *nothing changes if nothing changes* and *time does not heal all*.

What Can You Do to Grow in Grace?

If you're pregnant, you make time out of our busy schedules for frequent doctor appointments, and you find the money in your budget to cover his fees. Or, if you don't have enough, you see a less expensive doctor or borrow the funds from your parents. Sometimes you set up payment plans.

Then you buy saltines and 7-Up to help you through your morning sickness. When your belly begins to bulge, you spend more money on maternity clothes, or you borrow from friends.

You race to the library or bookstore and read as many books as you can on pregnancy, being a mother, and how to handle your family while this is all going on. You explain it to your loved ones and ask for their patience. If you have young children, you begin to teach them about babies. You try not to push yourself too hard and you try to take lots of naps.

Why then, when you have emotional problems, do you refuse to spend one cent on a doctor? Why do you say you can't afford counseling, or that you don't need it? You may even call educated, godly therapists "quacks" as an excuse to avoid change. Why do you say you don't have the time in your busy schedules? Why do you wait and hope it will just take care of itself?

Why do you pay dentists to fix your teeth, doctors to cure your ills, beauticians to fix your hair and nails, mechanics to fix your cars, dancers to teach your children ballet . . . but hesitate to pay someone to help heal your mind and emotions?

Why do you buy magazines to teach you fashion, cookbooks to give you recipes, tapes to provide music . . . but spend nothing on magazines, books, or tapes on emotional growth or relationships?

Perhaps you just never thought of it that way. Or perhaps you're fearful of the mess inside, stubborn, afraid to admit your faults, lacking in trust that it will work, a little prideful, or just plain lazy. Author Eric Ludy once said we don't invite God into our living room because we know he'll rearrange the furniture . . . or worse, he'll want *us* to rearrange some of our own furniture.

*Y*ou Are Precious

Your mind and emotions are just as precious as your body and spirit. They were created by God to be beautiful, and he has given you charge over them. He wants you to be good stewards over your body, mind, emotions, and spiritual life as well as your money. If you love yourself as he loves you, you will put the same effort into healthy deliveries of you problems as you do into healthy delivery of your baby. You need to love yourself as much as you love your children . . . nurturing yourself, learning what medication to take when you're emotionally sick, and not hesitating to take yourself to the doctor when an emotional fever hits. If you love yourself, you will be as gentle and as diligent in your after-care program as you would with any other physical problem.

Is anything stopping you from changing your life for the better? What fears might be holding you back? By reading this book, you've already shown a willingness to change. Keep up the good work!

What Does My Fear Say?

Change is hard—too hard. It's frightening. It doesn't feel good. Why can't I just accept things as they are? Why can't God see I'm doing the best I can? Things aren't that bad, really. Are they? This pain will go away over time, right?

What Does My Faith Say?

I will not view change as a huge, overwhelming process. If I feel like I can't change, I will change course and that can happen with one single step in a new direction. God promises to send me all the grace I need.

Love Letter

DAUGHTER,

Leave to me those who have hurt you. I want you to know how much I love them despite what they have done or failed to do. Do you realize that they also have been deeply hurt and scared, and that's part of the reason they hurt others? Can you look past your pain and see them as I do? I want you to let go of your resentments and fears and let me take over from here.

Do you trust me?

Your Loving Father

∾ 18 ∾

Granting Forgiveness

On Sunday evening Nancy's ex-husband showed up late—again—in bringing their children home after weekend visitation. After dinner she gave the kids a bath, tucked them in bed, and then settled onto the sofa with a cup of hot tea. Nancy turned on the TV and clicked through the channels until she found something she liked, and then, rolling up her sleeve, she tied the rubber tourniquet around her upper arm. Nancy reached out with her other hand, grabbed the small plastic syringe, and stuck it between her teeth. With her free hand she tapped lightly until her blood showed blue in her ready vein. Nancy stuck the needle in gently, shut her eyes, and squeezed. The familiar feeling rushed through her as she undid the tie, rolled her sleeve back down, sipped her tea, and pulled the cotton throw over her feet. The television show, "Touched by an Angel," was just starting, and Nancy was feeling better.

Nancy is a junkie. She injects herself every day with a substance that has robbed her eyes of clarity, her face of youth, and her life of joy. She doesn't want to face reality, so she uses the substance to make her feel better. Sadly, as long as she uses it, not only is she slowly heading toward death, she is blocking her body from receiving any reparative benefits. The healthy food she eats, the walks she takes, and the vitamins she pops are all useless while the

157

drug courses through her veins. The drug that is killing her is unforgiveness.

According to the world, Nancy has every right to refuse to forgive. Her ex-husband had a series of affairs, he lied for years (and still does), he lost their retirement, left her and the children financially strapped, and, on top of everything else, he gave her an incurable sexually transmitted disease. Nancy had been a good wife and did not deserve one bit of what happened to her. By holding onto her unforgiveness, however, she is hurting herself more than her ex-husband ever did.

Withholding forgiveness hurts us emotionally, physically, and spiritually. Father Bill Faella, a Catholic priest who has a healing ministry and works with recovering addicts in the Palm Springs, California area, says someone once told him, "Refusing to forgive is like swallowing poison and hoping the other person will die." What a perfect picture of how resentment destroys us. Or imagine we're cruising up and down the grocery store aisles, pushing our shopping carts with one hand and our mobile drip IV stands with the other. When we hold onto our resentment, we continually infuse ourselves with mental, emotional, and spiritual poison. Forgiveness allows us to pull out the needle.

Why Do We Find It So Hard to Forgive?

One reason we resist forgiving is that we don't really understand what forgiveness is or how it works. We think we do, but we don't.

Most of us assume that if we forgive our offenders, they are let off the hook—scot-free—and get to go about their merry ways while we unfairly suffer from their actions. We also may think that we have to be friendly with them again, or go back to the old relationship. While God commands us to forgive others, he never told us to keep trusting those who violated our trust or even to like being around those who hurt us.

The first step to understanding forgiveness is learning what it is and isn't. The next step is giving yourself permission to forgive and forget, letting go of the bitterness while remembering very clearly your rights to healthy boundaries.

$\mathcal{G}$ranting Forgiveness

- *Forgiveness is not letting the offender off the hook.* We can and should still hold others accountable for their actions or lack of actions.
- *Forgiveness is returning to God the right to take care of justice.* By refusing to transfer the right to exact punishment or revenge, we are telling God we don't trust him to take care of matters.
- *Forgiveness is not letting the offense recur again and again.* We don't have to tolerate, nor should we keep ourselves open to, lack of respect or any form of abuse.
- *Forgiveness does not mean we have to revert to being the victim.* Forgiving is not saying, "What you did was okay, so go ahead and walk all over me." Nor is it playing the martyr, enjoying the performance of forgiving people because it perpetuates our victim role.
- *Forgiveness is not the same as reconciling.* We can forgive someone even if we never can get along with him again.
- *Forgiveness is a process, not an event.* It might take some time to work through our emotional problems before we can truly forgive. As soon as we can, we should decide to forgive, but it probably is not going to happen right after a tragic divorce. That's okay.
- *We have to forgive every time.* If we find ourselves constantly forgiving, though, we might need to take a look at the dance we are doing with the other person that sets us up to be continually hurt, attacked, or abused.
- *Forgetting does not mean denying reality or ignoring repeated offenses.* Some people are obnoxious, mean-spirited, apathetic,

or unreliable. They never will change. We need to change the way we respond to them and quit expecting them to be different.

- *Forgiveness is not based on others' action but on our attitude.* People will continue to hurt us through life. We either can look outward at them and stay stuck and angry, or we can begin to keep our minds on our loving relationship with God, knowing and trusting in what is good.

- *If they don't repent, we still have to forgive.* Even if they never ask, we need to forgive. We should memorize and repeat over and over: forgiveness is about our attitude, not their action.

- *We don't always have to tell them we have forgiven them.* Self-righteously announcing our gracious forgiveness to someone who has not asked to be forgiven may be a manipulation to make them feel guilty. It also is a form of pride.

- *Withholding forgiveness is a refusal to let go of perceived power.* We can feel powerful when the offender is in need of forgiveness and only we can give it. We may fear going back to being powerless if we forgive.

- *We might have to forgive more than the divorce.* Post-divorce problems related to money, the kids, and schedules might result in the need to forgive again and to seek forgiveness ourselves.

- *We might forgive too quickly to avoid pain or to manipulate the situation.* Forgiveness releases pain and frees us from focusing on the other person. Too often when we're in the midst of the turmoil after a divorce, we desperately look for a quick fix to make it all go away. Some women want to "hurry up" and forgive so the pain will end, or so they can get along with the other person. We have to be careful not to simply cover our wounds and retard the healing process.

- *We might be pressured into false forgiveness before we are ready.* When we feel obligated or we forgive just so others will still like us, accept us, or not think badly of us, it's not true forgiveness—it's a performance to avoid rejection. Give yourself permission to do it right. Maybe all you can offer today is, "I

want to forgive you, but right now I'm struggling emotionally.
I promise I will work on it."

- *Forgiveness does not mean forgetting.* It's normal for memories
to be triggered in the future. When thoughts of past hurts occur,
it's what we do with them that counts. When we find ourselves
focusing on a past offense, we can learn to say, "Thank you,
God, for this reminder of how important forgiveness is."

- *Forgiveness starts with a mental decision.* The emotional part
of forgiveness is finally being able to let go of the resentment.
Emotional healing may or may not follow quickly after we
forgive.

When We Use Forgiveness to Feel Superior

A divorced woman had been the victim of an affair. In her bitterness,
she often referred to the other woman as the whore. She worked on
her healing from the tragedy and shared with a support group: "With
the grace of God, I have forgiven my ex-husband and the other
woman. I call her his mistress now because I see that other label just
showed my bitterness. I see now that they are in desperate need of
God and I pray for them all the time. They really need his help."

At first that might sound like this woman has reached a place
of true forgiveness. Just under the surface, though, we can still see
hurt and bitterness. Her focus is still fixed intently on the other
people. One of the true measures of forgiveness is that we let go
emotionally of the need to keep thinking and talking about the
other person(s). We hand them completely over to God's love and
care, not to God's condemnation. We also realize that we are just
as much in need of forgiveness as they might be. This divorced
woman had made some progress, but full forgiveness would result
in her being able to call the mistress by her given name.

After years of counseling and working through her own emotional
issues, the woman eventually came to a place of understanding how
we all have the same needs, we all can fail, and we all can grow

up without the tools needed to make healthy decisions. Then she completed the process of forgiveness. This time she shared, "I thank God he let me see that Dave and Sally are just like me and I'm just like them, and that he will take care of us all!"

Have *you* ever felt slightly self-righteous and superior because you forgave someone? As you grow in understanding and maturity, you may continue to forgive on different levels. That's part of the process.

Seeking Forgiveness and Forgiving Ourselves

Forgiving someone else is only the first step. We often need to seek forgiveness for our own actions or attitudes, and we need to lovingly forgive ourselves.

When my husband left, I was hurt, angry, and bitter. Although he certainly had violated me and our marriage, I had learned how important it was for me to get my focus *off of his actions* and back *on my own attitude*. I was tempted to feel superior to him and to look at how he sinned against me. As is common, I found myself attacking his character when I talked with my girlfriends.

There's a difference between talking with a counselor about the facts and feelings of the divorce and running around town sharing *his* faults and failures with others. Everything you say may be true, but does it really need to be repeated? Do you need to tell your children how weak their father is? How many times does your mother need to hear what a jerk he was? Do you need to focus longer than necessary on the hurts and tragedy? A time and a limit should be put on the woundedness, hurt, and anger. When we hold onto the feelings, as normal and natural as they are, and let them infect our relationships with our ex, the children, or mutual friends, then we have more to forgive—we need to seek forgiveness for our own failings.

This word picture might help: What if someone kidnapped you, tied you down, and shot you up with drugs, turning you, against your will, into a junkie? As the victim, of course you could blame them for your problem and work on forgiving them. They, in fact, *are* responsible for what happened to you, no question. But what if you, personally, kept on shooting up even in the days ahead, refusing to go to the rehab clinic to get counseling and refusing to let the doctors prescribe medication to help free you from addiction. Yet, you told everyone in town how the kidnappers ruined your life? Even when victimized, you can make things worse for yourself when you hold onto resentment and then refuse to forgive.

Pick up the phone or write a letter and ask forgiveness for your own attitude. True humility can be more freeing than forgiving the other person.

Reconciliation

If there is even the slightest chance of reconciling your marriage, you owe it to yourself, your ex-husband, and your children to make every effort toward that end. However, it may be that that point has passed for you. A marriage can be reconciled only if two people are fully willing to do whatever it takes. If your ex-spouse is not willing, you can do nothing further except work on your own healing.

Even though reconciliation of the marriage may not be possible, reconciliation of the relationship always has a chance. Remember, any reconciliation takes *two* and it takes *time*. It may not happen now or ever, but we should always leave the door cracked in case our ex-spouse, family members who hurt us, or even the person with whom he had an affair comes knocking on our door seeking forgiveness.

The Benefits of Forgiveness

Everyone is familiar with the Lord's Prayer. Sometimes we say it without thinking of the words, but the primary benefit of forgiveness is clearly laid out in ". . . forgive us our debts as we forgive our debtors . . ."(Matt. 6:12). In other words, while God fully forgives all our sins through Christ (Col. 2:13-14), we do not *experience* his forgiving grace when we fail to fully forgive others. We're like Nancy, who injected herself with the poison of unforgiveness; this poison blocks all the healing powers available to us.

Forgiveness frees us from guilt. Forgiveness cuts the emotional energy cord that constantly drains us. It frees us from a host of health problems that result from bitterness. Forgiveness is all about us and nothing about them. Forgiveness is a gift we give ourselves.

How to Forgive

Forgiveness puts us back in power and gives us control over the situation. Being empowered is one of the current feminine buzz-words in self-help books, in magazines, and on TV talk shows. These simple steps will remind you how to regain your real power:

P—Process your emotions. The first step in forgiveness is getting your focus off the other person's action and back on your own attitude.

O—Offer understanding. Be willing to understand that people who hurt have been hurt themselves.

W—Will to forgive, even if the feelings come and go. Make the mental decision and ask God to give you the grace to follow through emotionally.

E—Expect future offenses and take steps to insulate yourself. Don't stay a victim, and adopt more realistic expectations of others.

R—Reconcile if possible. Make one sincere attempt and then don't push it if the other person is not ready. Be prepared to wait years, if necessary. It's never too late.

What Does My Fear Say?

Sometimes I'm afraid that if I forgive others they'll think I'm weak and take advantage of me again. Sometimes I'm afraid that they won't have to suffer like I did, and that's just not fair! Sometimes I rush too quickly to forgive because I worry what others will think. I want to look good and I want my offenders to look bad.

What Does My Faith Say?

I don't need to worry about justice not being done. God promises that he will take care of all injustice. I don't need to worry what others think, and I don't need to worry about having to return to the same old relationship. I am free to forgive and still take care of myself, knowing God will take care of me.

SECTION

 III

Establishing New Priorities

Love Letter

PRECIOUS ONE,

Rest now, for yourself, and enjoy what I have prepared for you. Delight in my banquet, spices, and perfumes, and let my wine gladden your heart. Take time away from the crowd and go to a quiet place. Let your friends anoint you; let others wash your feet. Let yourself be loved as I love you.

Your Loving Father

19

You

In ancient times, a king placed a large boulder right in the middle of a well-traveled roadway. Then he hid himself and watched to see if anyone would remove the rock. Some of the kingdom's wealthiest merchants and stateliest courtiers came by and simply walked around it. Many loudly blamed the king for not keeping the road clear, but no one did anything to get the stone out of the way.

On approaching the boulder, a sturdy peasant woman with three children laid down her burden and tried to move the stone to the side of the road. She decided that moving the rock would make passage easier for her and safer for her children. After much pushing and straining, she finally succeeded. With the road clear, she began to gather her children and her load. Then she noticed a purse in the dirt that had been covered by the rock. The purse contained many gold coins and a note from the king indicating the gold was for the person who took the time to work to remove the rock from the road. The peasant woman learned what many divorced women never understand: every obstacle in life presents an opportunity to improve one's condition.

Can you see how the king is like God? He will reward our efforts at tackling the tough mental and emotional issues that face us during and after divorce. Clearing the road, instead of walking around our problems, will make life easier for us, and safer for our children, and will enrich us in countless ways.

Do you want to go for the gold? Are you ready to start real healing? Now that you've read through the types of *pain* that might plague you on your path past divorce, and the *principles* that are at work in your life, you can start to set healthy *priorities*. The very first priority is you.

Knowing When to Put Yourself First

Some of us have trouble putting ourselves first, which may be because:

- Since childhood, we've allowed our self-image to be damaged by others (*emotional energy thieves*).
- We're worried that God or others will think we're selfish (*fear of rejection*).
- We don't love, forgive, or accept ourselves (and our needs) unconditionally, as God does *(false guilt)*.
- We feel safer in a victim mentality or martyr role (*fear of taking ownership of our lives*).
- We like the feeling of pride that comes with being so humble.

Maybe this story can shed a little light on your current perception of yourself:

After a devastating fire in Yellowstone National Park, a forest ranger discovered a dead bird petrified in ashes, perched statuesquely at the base of a charred tree. Somewhat sickened by the eerie sight, he knocked the bird over with a stick. When he struck it, three tiny chicks scurried out from under their dead mother's wings. The loving mother, keenly aware of impending disaster, had carried her offspring to the base of the tree and gathered them under her wings, instinctively knowing that smoke would rise. She could have flown to safety, but had refused to abandon her babies, remaining steadfast as the flames scorched her small body.

When I first read this I sighed. Not only does it show a mother's heart for her babies, it is a beautiful picture of God's love for us, that he would take us under his wings and die for us. Then I started thinking about motherhood, and how noble it would be to literally die for our children. I think we moms would sacrifice our lives for our loved ones, without hesitation, in a heartbeat. The only problem is, we don't have to!

With a society that, in the past thirty years, has deified children to the point they come first in everything, we've created a terrible imbalance in the family. Parents no longer take care of themselves in healthy ways. Instead, their first priority is to give their time, energy, and money to whatever the children not only need but also want. There's a gross misunderstanding that a parent's role is to *provide* and *protect*, leaving out the third task: to *prepare*.

Preparing our kids for the real world means saying no, holding them accountable, teaching them delayed gratification, self-control and self-discipline, balance, and common courtesy. That means sometimes we don't provide or protect, instead allowing them, even from the time they are small, to go without, to fail, to step aside for another family member, to give up their own way, to pitch in and help, to do without expecting anything in return, and to put others first.

At times, children should definitely *not* come first, such as when you have had a hard day and a pounding migraine. Even though you promised to take them out for pizza, they may have to eat peanut butter and jelly at home. I'm not minimizing the importance of keeping promises, but let's get rid of the false guilt and fear of rejection that keeps us from having healthy boundaries.

Too many of us are caught up in pity for our children, especially after divorce, and we want so much to ensure they have the childhood we didn't have. So we drag ourselves out the door, head throbbing and temper flaring, when we need to put ourselves first and stay home in that bubble bath! In the long run, taking care of yourself first will make you a much better mother; you'll have the energy to teach, discipline, and prepare your children to have much more realistic expectations of the world. Children who realize that the world does not revolve around them will be better employees, friends, and husbands or wives.

During and after a marriage that resulted in divorce, the balance that was lost must be brought back to each family member, starting with the parents. Because children are too young and emotionally immature, parents need to guide them along the road to adulthood. If we're not in good mental and emotional shape, we will make lousy leaders.

You also may have a lot of work ahead in the ongoing legal, financial, and communication issues with your ex-spouse. To be ready to move these rocks as they appear along the path, keep up your mental, emotional, physical, and spiritual strength. Here are suggested steps to take in these four areas:

*F*ind Your PASSION

To stay mentally awake and on top of things, every women needs to work at or do something that's deeply satisfying. If you're employed, look at the areas in your job that bring you the greatest joy: working with people, the beauty of balancing numbers, or developing overall plans. Work with your employer or coworkers to change parts of your job that are draining, and build up those areas you find satisfying. If necessary, consider a job change.

Have you always wanted to go back to school? Even if it seems impossible and you have no time or money, start reading books in the subject you love. Some colleges offer scholarships or government grants for single moms. Maybe you need to focus on the kids for a few years, but you'll be surprised how those years will fly by, and you can at least be taking baby steps. It's almost humanly impossible to avoid bitterness if you do nothing to pursue growth during. Create long-term and short-term plans. This will help you feel less deprived, frustrated, and depressed. Without a vision, the people perish.

Many of the women I've talked to at seminars and in the DivorceCare groups have awakened their passions. They love to share what has worked for them, including taking one class per semester, learning a second language, preparing for and teaching Sunday school, and taking computer classes. Maybe some of their ideas will inspire you:

"I went into therapy and started learning about what makes people tick. After five years of schooling, I got my masters and am now a crisis counselor in a hospital!"—*Ronda*

"I went back to school to get my degree. I don't know what I will do with it, but it feels good!"—*Dodi*

"While taking quilting classes, I found something that really turns me on! I look forward to creating my quilts, which I give as presents to friends and family."—*Charlotte*

*F*igure Out Your PERSONALITY

Florence Littauer's personality teachings are my most practical and powerful tool for loving my neighbor as I love myself. Being Sanguine, my emotional needs are a little bit different from others'. While we all need to be loved and appreciated, Sanguines need lots of hugs and kisses, close physical touch, and someone to talk to, even more than the other temperaments do. As a single woman living alone, I have no physical touch, so I make sure to hug the neighbor's kids and keep my regular appointments for manicures and pedicures. It may sound simple, but having someone hold my hands and rub my feet helps keep me from getting depressed. My work can keep me isolated, so I make sure I get out at least once a day to visit the video store or the gas station. There I exchange greetings and jokes with the clerks and attendants. Monthly lunch with the girls also is a must for me.

While the opposite Melancholy personality can hole up contentedly for weeks in some laborious project, elbow deep in detail, I would go nuts! Yet, you might not like people hugging you all day and you may crave isolation, peace, and quiet. If that's the case, and you have a busy office and noisy kids, you'll need to take steps to get that much-needed quiet time!

Meeting your own emotional needs is like taking antibiotics to ward off depression. Below is a table based on Littauer's popular personality teachings. See what category you fall into:

Popular Sanguine

Basic Desire —Have Fun

Emotional Needs —Attention, Affection, Approval, Acceptance

Needs to be around people, have an audience and someone to talk to

Powerful Choleric

Basic Desire —Take Charge

Emotional Needs —Loyalty from the troops, Appreciation, Credit for Hard work, Sense of Control

Needs order, not chaos, and thrives on projects, big or small, the more the better

Perfect Melancholy

Basic Desire —Have Perfection

Emotional Needs – Sensitivity, support, space, silence

Needs to be doing something of value, like teaching or helping

Peaceful Phlegmatic

Basic Desire —Have Peace

Emotional Needs—Peace and quiet, lack of pressure, respect, feelings of worth

Needs to watch TV, take long naps, and just do nothing

---

*F*it in PLAY Time

Keeping yourself physically balanced means no more excuses for not walking fifteen or twenty minutes after dinner. Okay, maybe Midwest tornado warnings are the exception. Walking also enables some temperaments to meet their emotional needs for space and silence. Walking, running, dancing, or participating in sports is essential for keeping yourself in good shape so you can deal with the bumps ahead. Sometimes we do all the mental, emotional, and spiritual work we can and still feel down or depressed because we're packing on a few extra pounds, or not eating or sleeping well. Exercise helps our bodies to carry us through the tough times, and it releases the feel-good endorphins, which reward our hard work.

I dragged myself to Jazzercise on days when I thought I had no energy. After I got there, saw all my friends, started moving and getting my heart beating a little faster, I no longer felt like the world would end because I had no husband, no family, and no money. Okay, I admit it . . . when we did those kicks I did some special visualization that released a lot of tension.

*F*all on Your Knees in PRAYER

I've had it up to here with the fake spirituality depicted in the women's television shows and magazines. I'm tired of being told that certain physical actions are a form of spirituality. For instance, lighting incense isn't spiritual; it's physical. It's soothing and appealing to our sense of smell and can thus bring us to a place of physical pleasure and emotional peace. Sipping herbal teas, lighting candles, and contemplating the cosmos are physical, emotional, and mental practices that help clear us for spiritual connection, but in themselves are *not* spiritual. They are ritual.

Women's sites on the Internet address how to remember your spirit with martial arts, meditation, and mantras such as "I am wonderful, I am powerful, I love myself". While I am a firm believer in affirmations, I can't subscribe to self-talk that leaves out God. I know I am not always wonderful and powerful, because I am human. And on days I don't feel like I love myself very much, thank God I know *he* loves me even if I don't.

Our inner spirit is the part of us in which God dwells: The One True God . . . all of him . . . all his love . . . all his power. The spirit is not about our nose, our taste buds, or our breathing, but about the almighty, everlasting, Creator of the universe.

True spirituality then is about our awareness of, connection with, and relationship to God; it need not involve the physical or emotional. Spirituality is evidenced in our knowing him, loving him, and serving him.

If rooted in a relationship with God, special practices, diets, or ritual can be part of our whole-body experience of him, beautifully enhancing our relationship with the Lord. *But ritual without relationship is empty.*

The quickest way to get in touch with our spiritual side is prayer. Prayer is communication between two beings in relationship—not me-down-here and higher-power-out-there. Prayer is one of the easiest spiritual practices we can do any place, any time, any way.

When I was young, my father told me the story of two priests who were strolling through the garden after dinner. The younger one asked the much older priest, who was smoking a pipe, "Father, is it acceptable to smoke while you pray?"

"Oh, no!" the old priest gently rebuked the younger. "Prayer is reverent and we should always have the utmost honor and respect when we pray."

After thinking about it a minute, the younger priest then asked, "Father, is it all right to pray while we smoke?"

The old priest smiled. "Ahh-hh . . . *yes!*" he answered. "It is a joy to God that we pray to him at all times and in all places."

When I was younger I wanted my prayer life to be special and reverent, and, being human, I never found enough time to do it right. My dad was telling me that while ritual prayer time is pleasing to God, so is any other time and any other way. I didn't need to stop and try to find or make the time. I already had the time. Right then, right there. To this day I often find myself on automatic pilot at my Jazzercise class, dancing up a storm with my body, releasing tension and stress, while my mind is far away in prayer with God. Is it okay to pray while we dance . . . or drive, or work, or bathe, or change diapers or sheets, or sit in seminars and business meetings? *Yes!* Our Heavenly Father wants us to come to him at all times and in all places.

Other Ways to Care for Ourselves

When I asked women how they took care of themselves after divorce, the most common remedies included: Bubble baths, lunches with friends, weekly support groups, shopping, reading, extra naps, chocolate, good recreational reading, going to the gym, changing poor eating habits, repainting the bedrooms, gardening, sewing, singing, playing old CDs . . . even motorcycle riding.

After a period of grieving, some of these women also gave themselves permission to slowly start dating again. To many, this can be frightening. Some women, however, adamantly refuse to bring another man into their children's lives, focusing all their time, attention, and love on the kids. They put off loving themselves until the kids are gone. When the kids finally leave, these women may be isolated, introverted, and lonely, or cold, hard, and bitter. Other women shut down that part of their lives because it's easier and they don't want to risk getting hurt again. Each woman must decide if and when dating is best for her.

We have to be careful not to hide in our roles of motherhood or give the kids power over our adult social lives. The path of healing from the disappointment of divorce and the choices we make will be different for each of us. The key is maintaining balance in all areas of our lives, keeping our expectations consistent with reality, and avoiding bitterness, a sometimes difficult, but not impossible, task.

Let's follow King Solomon's example and, even if we have all the riches in the world, still pray for wisdom . . . one of the most precious coins in the purse God has for us.

What Does My Fear Say?

I'm not comfortable with taking care of myself. I'm afraid that I will be too selfish or that I will not be the best mother I can be. I worry that my children, who already have suffered greatly from the divorce, will be further damaged if I don't do everything I can to help them. If I can't keep a marriage together, then I will be the best mother I can be . . . even if it kills me.

What Does My Faith Say?

I need to trust God more and be willing to rest beneath his wings. I can trust that he will teach me, guide me, and take even better care of my children than I ever could. I will take time out for me and not fear making my children upset or hurt or angry. I'll see the bigger picture and realize that I still can be a loving, leading influence in my children's, and their children's lives, until the day I die.

Love Letter

MY BELOVED,

In marriage you became one flesh with your husband and now you have been torn in half. Do you know that I designed marriage that way to show you how deeply and lovingly I hold you? When you are in me, I am in you. I am love, and when you abide in me, I will abide in you. Stay with me, my precious daughter. I will help you from being ripped apart and will make you whole again.

Your Loving Father

20

Your Ex

*O*ccasionally I'll hear Taylor Dane's song "I'll Always Love You" on the car radio or pass the romantic restaurant where my ex-husband proposed and, for a moment, I'll think tender, bittersweet thoughts of the man who was mine. As I write this chapter, I know I'll never forget the times we laughed and played, fought battles together, stood side-by-side in raising his son, and shared a warm and loving marriage bed. I'm both sad and relieved that his smell, his taste, and his touch have faded in my memory. At other times, though, I could just kick him for what he did. Today we care about each other, and he makes sure I get to visit my stepson as much as possible. We've forgiven, but neither of us ever will forget. That's human nature.

Some women are such "good friends" with their ex-husbands that they can still share hugs; others fight the urge every day to shoot their ex, stick his body in the car, and drive it off a cliff. Some swing back and forth between the two. How you respond to the man who shared your bed, fathered your children, and promised to love you forever will be a natural outgrowth of your own emotional healing from divorce.

Even if you get along fine with your ex today, don't fool yourself into thinking you will always get along in the future . . . especially if and when he remarries, has new children, moves, or has a substantial change in his income.

How Women Are Getting Along with Their Ex

When women are asked to describe their relationship with their ex-husband, their responses range from still fighting or a cool, civil politeness to genuine caring and "brotherly" love.

"We do not get along. He is rude and hostile. He lies every chance he gets. Either that or he's sickeningly sweet and then erupts at the drop of a hat. It's impossible to talk to him. Thank God for Caller ID so I know what to expect when I pick up the phone."—*Serafina*

"I have two ex-husbands. My first ex and I do not get along at all. He refuses to talk to me, even about our daughter. I think I could get along with him if he would try, but he won't. My second ex and I don't talk either. He still intimidates me and for some reason I used to find myself not saying what I really felt, hoping to just ease him through the conversation and not hurt his feelings. I really want to tell him how angry I still am and how much he has hurt me."—*Dawn*

"We are civil to each other but we don't talk much and he purposely keeps his whereabouts unknown to me. I know the town but that's all. He got in trouble with the law and has been dodging child support. There's nothing I can do." —*Julie*

"When I can deal with him directly, without any interference from his new wife, we get along great. We communicate only about our children." —*Rene*

"I don't have any contact with him. The last I heard, he's serving twelve years for sexual abuse of young boys in our church. I prefer to keep my distance. Most people around here don't even know us since I moved and took back my maiden name." —*Lori*

"We get along fine. If we run into each other it's fine. He calls about every six months (drunk, I think) wanting me to come over while his present wife is at work. Needless to say, I do not." —*Audrey*

"My ex and I are friends, but I do not get too close emotionally because I don't want to get hurt again. I'll admit that I try to be as friendly as possible all the time to secretly make him regret leaving me and probably also to keep him cooperating with me." —*Sharon*

"My husband and I have learned to get along very well and I can say we are friends. Mostly it's because we've both learned to forgive each other and not stay stuck in the past." —*Kim*

"I haven't seen him in ten years. When I knew he was getting married again, I sent him a card wishing him happiness. He was grateful for that. I knew if he didn't feel like I had forgiven him, he would have taken that into his new life, and so I kind of see it as my wedding gift to both of them. Then I closed the door to the past." —*Gina*

"My ex always will have a special place in my heart. It had been many years since he'd left and I hadn't seen or heard from him. In 1992, over about a four-year period, I felt a tremendous burden to pray for him. This turned into a powerful passion, almost like a fire. I didn't know why. One day my father called to tell me he had just read in the obituaries that John had died. When I called his parents, I found out four years earlier he had been diagnosed as HIV positive. They told me he'd turned his life to God and spent his last few years ministering to young men struggling with homosexuality. It was a real comfort to think that, in my praying, I was part of that." —*Eva Marie*

Your relationship with your ex-husband can change over time and, like any relationship, depends on both people. All you can control is your own attitude. Based on what has worked for hundreds of ex-wives, these tips can help you learn how to respond lovingly and not react emotionally:

$\mathcal{J}$f You Still Don't Get Along

Rethink Your Expectations. He's not your husband. Don't expect him to still take care of you or be loving to you. Realistic expectations will help minimize your anger. Do you need to still grieve?

Keep Contact Short. If you argue, don't spend a lot of time with him, either in person or on the phone. Keep contacts to a minimum and communicate only about the children's health, safety, and welfare. Deal directly with him, not through the kids. Leave other family members out!

Don't Push Parenting on Him. If you don't think he has good parenting skills, or if he has different morals, don't try to coparent with him. Even though it's a father's responsibility, why keep expecting him to do something he can't or won't do? This only sets you both up for more fighting. If he is a good parent, work with him on that area and forget the rest. Make sure you are doing the best parenting job *you* can.

Write It Down. Write letters or notes if you have to communicate. It minimizes the tension, allows him time to process your requests or comments, and leaves a paper trail in case questions arise about dates or times. Learn to ask instead of tell. Reread your letters before you send them and take out all the angry words.

Don't Be Angry on Behalf of Your Kids. Don't do your children's anger work for them. You have enough anger of your own. If he lets them down, instead of attacking him, teach the kids how to handle their own hurts, fears, anxieties, or depression.

Get Smart. Buy a book or tape on communication skills. Learn to clarify what he says to you by repeating back what you think you heard. Learn to quietly hang up or walk away when the emotions flare. Remember that we don't have to attend every argument to which we are invited! And, we all can learn new tricks of talking so people will listen.

Protect Yourself and Your Family. Take the Cloud/Townsend course on *Boundaries* (available at bookstores). Learn to say, "I'm sorry, Vince, but that subject is not up for discussion," or "I'm hanging up now. When you have calmed down a little, please call me back or write me a letter, because I do want to hear what you have to say."

Stay Guarded. Remember you do not have to trust your ex-husband. Trust needs to be earned and learned. Trust God instead.

Take Your Own Inventory. Examine the fears that might underlie your anger or mistrust. Go back to what you know God has promised you. Evaluate whether or not you are starting the arguments or causing the conflict. Could you listen to your ex-husband's complaints with a more open mind and forgiving heart? Sometimes he might be right. Could you benefit from parenting classes yourself?

Step Back. Accept that sometimes you just will not get along, and don't obsess about it. Pray for him, but then get your focus off him and back onto your own attitude.

If You Get Along "Just Fine"

Don't Manipulate. Be careful that you are not using kindness to manipulate and stay in control.

Maintain a Healthy Separateness. Look for ways that you might be overstepping physical or emotional boundaries in an attempt to get close again or to make up for past problems.

Avoid Sex with the Ex. Guard your heart and your purity. As high as 40 to 55 percent of divorced women report having sex with their ex. It may be convenient and feel right, but it really is using each other to fill an empty place, and it eventually only drives the pain deeper into your soul. If you still have mutual feelings for each other, get into counseling to discuss reconciliation. If you don't want that, don't sleep with him. Trust God to grant you the desires of your heart in his time.

Catch Your Jealousy. Don't try to stake your legal territory by being overly friendly or throwing your weight around in front of his new love interest. He's not your husband any more. If he' s remarried, respect his new marriage.

Keep It Cool. Don't indulge in excessive displays of affection or act and dress seductively to keep him on your leash. It may mislead him and cause the children to hope even harder for a reconciliation that never will happen. After a difficult divorce, you may want to kiss and make up. Finding a comfortable new role with each other can be difficult. Although affection is a continuation of natural feelings and may make everyone feel better for the moment, it might not be fair to anyone.

Change Mythical Thinking. Don't assume he always will be there for you, whether or not you think he owes you. Expect nothing that he couldn't or wouldn't give in the marriage, or isn't giving you now.

Don't Blame the Other Woman. If he gets along with you alone, but there's trouble when his new wife gets involved, do not blame her. No man is that weak and no woman is that powerful. If he changes his position or attitude with you at different times, that is his choice and his responsibility. Triangulating (bringing a third person into the problem) or trying to keep the new woman out of the picture, reflects your own insecurity and fear of losing what you see as the power position. Appreciate him. Thank him when he is mature and cooperative. Pray for him.

The Good-Bye Ritual

Just as we say good-bye in a formal funeral ceremony, we need to find a way that works for us in closing the door to our marriage. Since the beginning of time, ritual has been a healing form of closure; we have good-bye parties at work, when school is over, and when we move. One woman shared with me that she gathered all her ex-husband's leftover mementos, photos, and gifts he had given her, wrapped them lovingly in a ribboned box and buried them in the backyard. She invited her girlfriends over and they shared tears, laughter, and a little wine over candlelight. "It was beautiful," she told me. "It helped me move ahead."

Writing your ex-husband a good-bye letter also helps to heal a broken heart and brings closure. The purpose of the letter is to tell him what you loved about him, what you will miss, and what you will *not* miss. By the time you are finished, the letter should be a clear, honest communication without attacking his character or trying to make him feel guilty. It can be a gift of love to you both.

Start by letting all your thoughts and feelings flow out into your letter. Hold nothing back. Then go back and read it to add anything you may have left out. Now read it again and do the following:

- Take out or reword any snotty, cold, angry, or accusatory words or phrases.
- Look for any ulterior motives in your writing and change it.
- Pretend you are your son or daughter and, as an adult, you are now reading the letter Mom wrote to Dad when they divorced.

Let the letter sit a day or two and re-read it. Share it with a counselor or trusted friend, but don't take it to everyone you know.

Send it to your ex-husband, with no expectation of a reply. If you don't know where he is, give it to your pastor, counselor, therapist, or friend, or stick it in a drawer until the kids grow up, and share it with them at the appropriate time.

What Does My Fear Say?

I'm afraid that I'll never get control back over my ex-husband or that he will continue to hurt me. Sometimes I worry that my guilt will come back to haunt me, so I need to stay overly friendly to make up for the past. Sometimes I miss him; sometimes I want to kill him! Sometimes I'm just glad he's gone.

What Does My Faith Say?

I know that God will take care of us both. I know I can learn new ways of looking at my ex as a friend or neighbor, and, if I can't trust him, I can at least see him as a stranger who deserves courtesy, honesty, and civil behavior. I know God will honor my efforts. If I'm glad he's gone, I will be grateful for a new chance in life and ask God to keep all bitterness out of my heart.

Love Letter

PRECIOUS ONE,

*I love you, but I love her too. You don't have to be her friend
or even like her. You don't have to trust her, but I want you to
trust me. I want you to open your heart to forgiveness and
know that I will take care of her . . . and I will take care of you.*

Your Loving Father

✌ 21 ✌

The Other Woman

Barbara was devastated when she found out her husband of twenty years had a three-year affair and was planning to marry his younger girlfriend as soon as the divorce was final. For the next few agonizing years, Barbara thrashed about on a sea of rage and depression. Her teenaged children seemed to be weathering the divorce much better than she was, so she finally decided to get some counseling. Working through her emotions, Barbara eventually came to a place of peace that allowed her to continue working, parenting, and enjoying her life, but with one exception. She still hated the other woman.

Even though her children went frequently to visit their father and his new wife, Barbara refused to speak her name. Before long, Barbara's oldest daughter, Marsha, came home and excitedly announced that Daddy and Cindy were going to have a baby. The news sent Barbara into a whole new emotional tailspin of depression. Barbara's heart had ached for another baby, but for the last few years before the divorce her husband had made it clear he wanted no more children. Now he was happily building a whole new family with "her."

As time passed, Barbara watched her children become attached to their new half-brother. Eventually the pain of hearing her children talk about little Joey and the fun they'd had at Dad's no longer was unbearable. Still, Barbara never acknowledged little Joey in conversation, and her children learned to avoid mentioning to her anything about their other life.

About ten years after the divorce, a sudden tragedy befell the family when Barbara's ex-husband dropped dead of a heart attack. When Barbara heard the news, she was flooded with old emotions. She attended the funeral for her children's sake, but refused to look at or speak to her children's stepmother and half-brother.

One night after the funeral, Barbara's daughter dropped by for dinner.

"Mom," sighed Marsha, "I really need to talk to you."

"Sure, honey, what's up?" asked Barbara.

"Mom . . ." Marsha began slowly, and then blurted out, "I think it's really rotten the way you have treated Cindy and Joey all these years!"

Barbara stiffened in her chair, leaned forward to meet her daughter's eyes, and replied tersely, "Young lady, how *dare* you speak to me about them! You have *no* right to . . ." Marsha reached out, grabbed her mother's arm, and, holding her gaze, interrupted.

"Mom, STOP! I know you were hurt. I know it was wrong. I know what Daddy did was terrible, but that was a long time ago. I need you to hear me on this."

Barbara could see her daughter's eyes brimming with moisture and heard the earnestness in her voice. She took a deep breath, let it out, sat back, and listened. "Okay."

"Mom, for years I have wanted to tell you about Dad and Cindy and Joey, but I knew it would hurt you. All of us kids knew you didn't want to hear it, so we never told you. But Cindy has been the sweetest, most loving stepmom we ever could have. I know this is hard for you to hear, but Daddy loved her a lot, and she was good to him. She used to make us our favorite dinners whenever we came over and she always knew how to get the boys to stop fighting. She helped me with boyfriend problems and helped the boys with their homework, just like you did. Cindy never said anything bad about you, and she was the one who told me to respect you when we used to fight about the car. Remember?"

Barbara listened quietly.

"Cindy's been good to us all these years, and we adore Joey. I wish you could know him, he is so cute and so smart! Mom . . . I know how you feel . . . this must be really hard for you . . . but, it's been hard for us, too . . ."

Marsha's voice cracked and tears fell freely now. Barbara's heart was moved, and she reached out for her daughter's hand. A moment of silence passed. Marsha wiped her eyes, blew her nose and continued strongly.

"Mom, Joey is our brother. I love him. When dad died he left you that big settlement from your old life insurance policy, right?"

Barbara wondered where this was going. She replied, "Yes honey, and other than you kids it's about the *only* good thing he did for me! It's going to get me through my retirement. Why?"

"Well." Marsha looked straight at her mother and said, "Cindy was left with nothing. I guess Dad never got any new life insurance for her and Joey, and he left a bunch of unpaid bills. Cindy has nothing, Mom . . . *nothing*. She's even going to lose their house."

It was all Barbara could do to not scream out, "Well that's exactly what he left *me* with ten years ago! It serves her right!" Instead, Barbara asked her daughter tersely,

"Marsha, what do you expect me to do?"

Marsha paused and said quietly, "Nothing, I guess, I mean . . . well, do what you want. I just wanted you to know the facts. I just wanted to tell you how I've been feeling all these years. I thought maybe you might be willing to help a little, that's all. I'm really, truly sorry this has been so hard on you."

For the next three days Barbara agonized over the conversation with her daughter. On Saturday morning she got up, poured herself a cup of coffee, and sat down at the breakfast table with stationary and a pen. On Monday, Cindy opened her mail and read the first communication she'd ever had from the woman whose husband she'd taken so long ago.

Dear Cindy,

I know you and I never have spoken, and this is the hardest letter I've ever had to write. You must know how I have felt all these years, and I don't think its necessary to dig up all that. My children have told me that you have always been a wonderful step-mother to them. They tell me you are a good mother to their brother, Joey. I understand when Dick died he left you with no insurance and no source of income to cover living expenses.

Dick and I had an old insurance policy that will keep me comfortable for the rest of my life. This letter is to inform you that I have instructed my attorney to deposit a regular income for you and Joey into your bank account each month until Joey is eighteen. My attorney will be contacting you. I would prefer it if you would please not call or contact me. This is very difficult for me and I don't know if I will ever be able to be your friend. But my children love you. Because you have taken care of my children's needs while they were with you these last ten years, I want to help you take care of your son.

Sincerely, Barbara

Although this true story has a happy ending, it is just a variation on a centuries-old theme: *females have been fighting over men forever*. The emotions that fly between feminine rivals are among the most powerful on earth, even spawning wars between nations. In the Old Testament, Jacob's first and second wives, Leah and Rachel, fought continuously over the affection, attention, and loyalty of the man they both had married. Bitterness grew with each new baby born to the other, as the two wives feared a loss of their position and power in the family tents. It's no different today. As a divorced woman, we may face the same fears that feed our own hurt, anger, or resentment toward the new woman in our ex-husband's life.

Getting Along for Control's Sake

It's not uncommon for some ex-wives and new wives (or girl-friends) to become friends and join forces in managing the new family units, especially when the husband is a passive personality and prefers that the women take care of the children. This may be preferable to both women, and keeps the husband happy, but this approach has pitfalls of its own:

- When the two women are the coparents, this relieves the father of his God-given responsibilities to connect with and lead his family. Women who don't trust their ex or new husband to properly parent the children will feel safer being in control, and the passive father will feel less pressure. The healthy bond that should be created between husband and wife in making parenting decisions together is transferred away from the marriage and develops between the two women.

- When mothers are the primary caretakers and decision makers, both boys and girls tend to grow up believing this unbalanced pattern is healthy. They expect dads to take the backseat and moms to be in control. Passing this dysfunctional pattern to the next generation is likely to result in their own future marriage problems.

- We can be lured into a false sense of friendship with the new woman, when in fact we may be using each other to feel in control and to keep informed of the other side.

- Because of the natural tendencies of women to bond, especially when raising children together, it can be tempting to pry into or share inappropriate intimacies. It's not wise to share emotional, sexual, financial, or other secrets that are none of the other person's business. This also violates the privacy of the new marriage.

- Another temptation is for the new wife and ex-wife to start husband-bashing. Emotional bonds in the female friendship can be healthy, but should be limited in scope and respectful of boundaries and never should diminish or threaten the new marriage.

- Even if the interaction between the women seem in the best interest of the children, anything that creates a triangle or pulls away from the marriage relationship is, in the long term, never in the best interest of anyone.

Facing Your Fears, Embracing Your Faith

If you're in a high-conflict situation or nursing bitterness toward your husband's new love interest, ask yourself, *What am I afraid of?* Fear lies beneath any of the negative emotions you have toward her. Now that you understand how to get rid of fears by replacing them with faith, let's examine some of the most common problems with the other woman:

What Does My Fear Say?	What Does My Faith Say?
What if my kids like her better than me?	*I know no one can ever replace that special place in a child's heart that is reserved just for his/her mother.*
What if they start calling her Mom?	*My kids need to feel comfortable when they are at their father's home. It doesn't matter how many people they call Mom; no one will ever take my place in their hearts.*
What if she says bad things about me or turns my children away from me?	*My children have been given free will just as we all have. If God allows them to have the freedom of feelings, I need to give them that same freedom. I have God's love, even if someday I lose my children's.*

*W*hat Does My Fear Say?	*W*hat Does My Faith Say?
What if she teaches my children something I don't believe in?	*Sometimes all I can control is the time I spend with my children. I will teach them well and learn to listen. I will encourage safe, open discussion of anything in our home.*
What if our friends or family take her side?	*God knows the truth about each of us. I don't need everyone to be on my side.*
What if my ex-husband is swayed by her influence?	*I won't fool myself into believing that I can always get him to agree to what I need or want, no matter who is influencing him.*
What if she pressures him to not send the money he owes?	*God will take care of my family's and my financial needs.*
What if she is younger, prettier, smarter, and succeeds in replacing me in his heart?	*I do not need to keep emotional ties with my ex-husband. I will learn to let go and complete the grieving process, trusting God to meet my emotional needs.*

Do you need to get your focus off her? Do you need to forgive her? Do you need to seek forgiveness for your own actions or attitude toward her? Don't let the other woman become an emotional energy thief who drains you of your joy in life. You already know how to unplug: face your fears and embrace your faith.

Love Letter

MY DAUGHTER,

Just as you named your own children, I have called you by name; you are mine. Your children are also mine. Don't be afraid any longer; be anxious for nothing when it comes to your babies. Put me first, and teach them the same, and I will take care of you all.

Your Loving Father

22

Your Kids

"But Mom, it's not fair!" I whined. I was ten years old and Mom had just taken away my doll.

Well, it wasn't really *my* doll. For Christmas my two sisters and I had received three identical dolls, all with adorable faces and long braided hair. The only difference was that mine had pink hair, Barb's doll had yellow, and Serena's had white. Every day after I made my bed, I would prop up my doll against the pillow, arrange her braids neatly, and make sure her dress was fluffed out, sitting her next to Tiny Tears and Pitiful Pearl. Because they were like my children, I loved my dolls and took very good care of them.

From the time I was very young I always had wanted to be a mother with lots of babies, just like Mom. Whenever one of my younger brothers or sisters would start to cry, I'd rush to them and try to be the best little mother I could be. I felt the same way about my dolls.

One day I was outside playing in our backyard with my brothers and sisters and noticed the dog chewing on something in a mud puddle. It was Serena's doll. In my usual big-sister (bossy) tone I advised Serena that her doll was in the mud. Serena never liked me telling her what to do, and apparently didn't care that her doll was the dog's dinner. So, I picked up the doll, took it to the bathroom and washed its hair and clothes. I sat her under Mom's bouffant hairdryer, fixed her braids, ironed her dress, and retied the ribbons. Then I put her on my bed next to her pink-haired sister and my other dolls.

For almost a year Serena's doll lived happily in my room. One day Serena came into my bedroom, as she had done hundreds of times before, but this time she announced, "That's *my* doll and I want it."

My motherly instinct leapt out like a lion. "No way! You don't deserve to have this doll because I'm the one who cleaned her, cared for her, and loved her more than you did. I deserve to have this doll. You don't. You just left her out in the yard. Get out of my room!"

Serena ran out, crying loudly, "M-O-M!"

I grabbed the doll in my arms and ran out to Mom to beat Serena to the punch.

"Mom, she left the doll outside and it got all dirty. She didn't care. I took the doll and cleaned it up and took care of it . . ." I appealed to Mom's sense of justice and her own sense of motherhood. I really didn't expect her answer.

"Honey, I know. But the doll is Serena's. It's not yours and never has been yours," said my mother.

"But Mom, she doesn't take care of it! It's not fair!"

"Rosie, I agree Serena should take care of her doll, but that doesn't mean she has to." I saw Serena gloat. "You can't make her do it the way you think she should. She doesn't come in here and tell you how to dress your dolls. I know it doesn't seem fair, but that's the way it is."

Then Mom added something that I'll never forget.

"Just because you take good care of something and love it doesn't make it belong to you."

It broke my heart, but I'll never forget Mom's words or the two basic principles I learned which all mothers going through divorce should understand:

1. *Our children are not really our own, they are God's.*

I heard someone once say that God doesn't send children *to* us, but *through* us, and only for a short time. If God intended our children to have independent minds, free will and eventually to have their own separate life in the world, and we are only care-takers for awhile, then all the more should we make the most of the precious time we have to prepare them for life. In their childhood and adolescent years, we often place too much emphasis on loving and nurturing them, taking them to ballet and soccer, and trying to make them happy. Sometimes we don't properly understand our parenting role, and we act too much as their nurse instead of their doctor. Nurses give suckers and colorful Band-Aids; doctors give kids painful shots and sometimes even have to cut them open. Nurses make kids smile; doctors make kids cry. Kids like nurses. Kids are scared of doctors.

That's why we sometimes fail to give our children the mental, emotional, and moral tools they will need—we don't want to make them cry. Yet, how will they survive a declining society, financial problems, and the highest risk in history of failing in their own marriages, especially since their parents divorced? We don't want them to fear us; we want them to like us. But if we don't take responsibility for doing the hard or painful things necessary to equip them for life, or if we are afraid to operate, then we risk losing their lives . . . emotionally and spiritually.

While school, sports, and lessons are important, divorced mothers should, more than ever, primarily focus on teaching their children to identify their emotions, learn communication skills, solve problems, set priorities, handle disappointment, and put their growing faith into practice. Of course we can't teach our children these things unless we take the time to heal and learn for ourselves.

2. *Just because you love your children and take good care of them doesn't mean they belong only to you. They have the right to know, love, and spend as much time as possible with their father, other family members, friends, and their community.*

When I lost Serena's doll, I dealt with the separation anxiety every mother faces when children start preschool, move out of the house, or are taken away by divorce. Even when we have primary custody, we may agonize over the time our children spend with another rightful parent through weekend visitation orders. We often fear that their father will not take as good care of them as we would, and perhaps we are right.

In the healing of our emotions regarding our children, God reminds us that he will take care of us, and he will take care of them. If we are worried, anxious, and fearful, that reveals our own lack of faith. Even if we have no faith in our ex-husband, we are to have faith in God.

I've heard the same stories over and over in our counseling sessions with divorced women: He doesn't feed them right. He doesn't drive carefully. He drinks in front of them. He lets them stay up too late. His girlfriend is a bad influence on my children. They don't go to church. They go to a weird church. He lets them see bad movies.

Of course we need to keep our eyes and ears open to situations that we can control and improve. We might be able to enlist the court's help in making the time spent with Dad better for the children. Most often, though, we have no power over that, and we need to learn to let go, grieve and come back to our Heavenly Father's arms. We must quit trying to play God, and put our faith into practice. As hard as it is to hear, some mothers who pride themselves on caring so much may be doing greater damage to their children in their overcontrol of the situation.

Unhealthy Childhood Roles

While you can't always control what happens at Dad's house, you can keep an eye out for the four most common mistakes moms make in their own homes. When Dad's absence creates a vacuum, mothers mistakenly put their children into one or more of these four unhealthy roles:

Adult—We "adultify" our children when we tell our sons they now must be the little man of the house, or our daughters that we'll need to lean on them now that Dad's gone. Hey, they are still kids! Tell your son you'll need some extra help now that Dad's gone, but don't put him in the position of the adult male. Because God made men to instinctively protect women, sometimes our boys naturally will try to take on the adult role. Although children of divorce will have to pull a little harder, be careful not to depend on them too much. Forcing children into adult positions only robs them of their childhood and teaches them to unnecessarily assume responsibility that God never intended them to have. Our children may become controlling and overburdened with a false sense of obligation in all areas of life. Anxiety, stress, and depression can follow, though be barely noticeable. Allow your kids to be kids. But don't go to the other extreme and let them off the hook and stay babies.

Baby—After divorce, part of us can feel like a hurt little baby and we may project that babying onto our children. We think they (and we) have suffered such great pain that we don't want to put on them any more discomfort or stress. We don't hold them accountable for age-appropriate responsibility and therefore not only are failing to prepare them for life, but we might be creating pitiful little victims or self-centered, whiny brats! We also like to keep them our babies because they bring such comfort to our own pains. Remember to balance your role as parent between nurse and doctor.

Companion—Kids can be a real comfort and help stave off loneliness, but we should resist the temptation to make them our companions and confidantes. I watched one divorced mother turn her only son into a surrogate spouse. From the time the boy was about six or seven years old, she took him everywhere with her, including to R-rated movies. In the evenings she let him sit on the sofa with her and watch adult-themed situation comedies on television. He listened in on her conversations with other adults about matters too intense for his young ears. When money was tight, she shared concerns about the budget with him to the extent he began to take on the worries of what would happen to them. He was her roommate, her friend, her dinner date, and her adult companion. Today, as a teenager, he struggles with guilt about naturally separating from mother, loving her and wanting to please her, but hating her and wanting to run away. Other emotional anxieties are surfacing, too. The seeds this mother is sowing will, indeed, be evidenced in problems in this boy's adult life.

Deity—By placing our kids above everything else, we might be making gods out of them. Many mothers, divorced or not, will throw themselves across the altar of self-sacrifice to their children, baring their bosoms to the sword of motherly martyrdom. There's a difference between a healthy prioritizing of children's mental, emotional, and physical needs, and putting them first in all situations. At times a child should not come first because it gives them a false sense of how and where they will fit into the world. When our world revolves around our children, they can become self-absorbed to the point of being unable to mature. They become their own god. They can become demanding, self-righteous, and even depressed when they discover the rest of the world does not hold them on a pedestal.

Part of preparing our kids for life is giving them a balanced sense of when they will have to wait, hold back, sit down, lose a turn, face unfair treatments, put others first, and delay their own gratification. Your kids should be able to voice their opinion and have it be considered, but they should not decide who you date, what car you buy, or what you cook for dinner. They should not make adult decisions about where to live or what to spend. Who's the head of *your* family?

And what is your focus? Have you ever heard a divorced mom say, "My kids are my life!"? Our life should first be our relationship with God and becoming the woman he wants. Don't put off a life for yourself until they are grown. It's possible to be a good mom and balance a personal life apart from the children in which sometimes they come last.

If you haven't built up a library of parenting books by now, it's time to start. After divorce, the best thing you can do for your children is to educate yourself on how to meet their unique and individual emotional needs, how to discipline effectively, and how to understand what they are really saying when they withdraw, attack, or sink into depression.

*I*s Divorce Really That Bad on the Kids?

Yes, it is. We recognize that, in many ways, divorce is worse than death. At least *we* have some adult reasoning to help us face the problems of a broken family. Children, though, do not have our maturity. Some experts say that for children, divorce is not only worse than death, it's like an ongoing nightmare from which they can't wake.

With her new book, *The Unexpected Legacy of Divorce: A 25-Year Landmark Study* (Hyperion Books), seventy-eight-year-old psychologist Judith Wallerstein has created a stir in the media about the tragic effects of divorce on children. This much-quoted, much-critiqued grandmother continues to shoot arrows into the hearts of parents who believe children will eventually get over divorce. She finds that adult children of divorce are so insecure that only 40 percent marry, and they have huge fears of loss, conflict, betrayal, and loneliness.

Wallerstein's primary contention is that, "The major impact of divorce does not occur during childhood or adolescence. Rather it rises in adulthood."[1]

She quotes adult children of divorce as saying, "My parents' divorce is with me every day." She says she is amazed "how much their parents' divorce shaped their adult years."[2]

*P*ermanent Scars Versus Permanent Wounds

Divorce isn't the only harm we can bring our children. Of course divorce hurts. Of course it damages the soul and causes fear, anxiety, and emotional problems. But so does a lot of other sinful human behavior. Everything harmful that we suffer in childhood eventuality plays itself out in adulthood. Controlling parents, emotionally absent parents, overly permissive parents, self-centered, angry, and insecure parents will pass on pain and emotional problems to their children. Like any slow-growing disease, the cancerous effects of poor parenting will be worse in adulthood if the child never learns to emotionally heal.

Divorce is not the only source of emotional wounds that affect children. My parents have been married fifty years. They went to church every Sunday and never divorced. I used to think we had a good childhood, but I now know that Mom and Dad never had developed the skills nor had the tools to meet all our emotional needs. Partly because of that, and partly because we all are imperfect humans in need of grace, today my siblings' adult families are plagued with divorce, drug use, alcoholism, addictions, depression, and more. There was no divorce in our childhood, but there always will be problems in our adult lives.

When divorce does occur, it does not necessarily mean the end. I do not intend to minimize the effects of divorce on children—the ripping apart of the family is devastating. It's painful. It's hell. But it's damage need not be permanent. In speaking with adult children of divorce, some of whom are in my own family, I've discovered that they still carry scars, but their wounds have been healed. Their parents spent time talking to them over the years, took them to professional counseling, and encouraged their continuing education in relationship issues. Children who were exposed to a healing and recovery program, much like I prescribe here for women, have successfully overcome most of the damage. Permanent scars need not be permanent wounds.

Wise mothers can take steps to help their children through the devastation of divorce. To help your children you might:

- Sign up for a children's support group through your church or community counseling center.
- Listen for their anxieties and take time to reassure them.
- Buy books written for children of divorce and spend time reading them together. For older children, let them read alone and then make time for discussion.

- Educate yourself about their deepest emotional needs. Just as we have different personalities and unique emotional needs, so do our children.
- Make sure they spend plenty of time with aunts, uncles, grandparents, and other loving and supportive relatives.
- Teach them what you have been learning about emotions, grieving, and acceptance. Teach them about their Heavenly Father.
- Take time once a day to stop and take their emotional temperature. "How can I be sensitive to you right now, Sweetie?" is like a magic pill for whatever is hurting a child. If they need a hug, give them two. If they need space and silence, let them have it with no pressure or guilt.

Children may never forget the divorce, but they *can* get over it. To say and believe otherwise is to say God is powerless. It says he is no help at all to our families. Children can be lead through the recovery process by a strong, caring mother and healed through the love and grace of God. Believe it.

What Does My Fear Say?

I fear for my children. I worry about them when they are with their father or with others. Sometimes I just don't know what to say to them. I'm afraid I am not enough to get them through this mess.

What Does My Faith Say?

His grace is sufficient for me! I can begin to make new priorities for my children and myself, one day at a time, one step at a time. He loves them more than I ever could, and I will entrust them to his care. I'll do my part and let go.

Love Letter

SWEET ONE,

Don't worry about losing money or finding injustice in the courts. Do what you can, but let go of any fear. Even though the world may fail you, trust that I will provide for you. You will never know in advance how I will make it happen, nor will I tell you.

Now look at the birds of the air, who don't have to work, grocery shop, or balance checkbooks, but I feed them! Look at the lilies of the field, how beautifully they are clothed. Don't you know that I love you far more than birds and will adorn you in all that you need so that you will be the most splendid of all flowers?

Your Loving Father

❧ 23 ❧

Money and the Courts

*I*s Ann Landers right when she says that *communication* and *money* are the two biggest problems in marriage and divorce?

Not really. If we couldn't keep food down because of the flu bug, we would not tell our friends, "Oh, I'm home sick with appetite problems." We'd tell them we had the flu. Just as your loss of appetite is a symptom of the flu virus, problems with money are a symptom of our mental and emotional state.

With financial difficulty after divorce, we often focus on the symptoms (our bank account) and fail to see the real underlying problem (our attitude). To illustrate, here's another little gem that's floating around the Internet:

One day a father and his rich family took his son to the country with the firm purpose of showing him how poor some people are. They spent a day and a night at the farm of a very impoverished family. When they got back from the trip, the father asked his son, "How was the trip?"

"Very good, Dad!"

"Did you see how poor some people are?" the father asked.

"Yeah!"

"And what did you learn?"

The son answered, "I saw that we have a dog at home and they have four. We have a pool that reaches to the middle of the garden; they have a creek that has no end. We have imported lanterns in our yard, but they have the stars. Our patio reaches to the property line but they have the whole horizon."

When the boy was finished, the father stood speechless. His son added, "Thanks, Dad, for showing me how poor we are!"

It's true. Money never is the problem. It's our attitude toward money that's the problem. Arguments over finances and property can extend for years after a divorce, centering around three main areas of concern: child support, spousal support, and division of property.

Child and Spousal Support

Battles over support are a common symptom. The real problem is fear of not being able to provide, lack of faith that God will take care of us, need for control, selfishness, and even revenge. Engaging in lengthy, legal warfare over child and spousal support often indicates a lack of appreciation for what we do have and a failure to accept the reality of our circumstances.

Money never is the real issue. Every human being should have a roof over his or her head, clothes on her back, a meal in her belly, and someone to love. After that, it's all extra. Do you realize how blessed we in our nation are to be able to take for granted not only those things, but also much more, every day of our lives? Thankfully, governments do all they can to ensure legally that children never will go without those basic human needs, but that does not guarantee that our children will receive the level of support that we as parents have come to expect . . . hope for . . . or think that our children deserve.

The failure of divorced women to accept this harsh reality, grieve over the loss, and put their faith back in God keeps them in angry bondage to bitterness.

All over the world, many women have to cut back financially, learn to go without, pull their children out of private school, cut off the cable TV, and serve their babies canned fruit cocktail for dinner. If your husband died and there was no insurance or no family to support you, you would have to change your financial way of life. No government on earth can guarantee every woman the right to be continually supported at the level to which she may have been accustomed.

If your husband lost his legs in a car accident and could never work again, you'd adjust to your new income levels. You might put your children in day care and go back to work. Even if you have no children or they are grown, you'd still face big changes in your economic lifestyle.

Any of these circumstances would be hard on you and your family. All of them would require you to complete the grieving process, starting at shock and denial, working through anger and guilt, plodding slowly through a mourning period, and finally coming to acceptance and release. You'd have to reach out for family support, assistance from the church, and help from your friends.

The choice is up to you. You can stay stuck at the greatest point of your pain by fighting for something that you may never get, or you can find freedom by letting go.

Even a Little Teabag Can Buy Happiness

After my divorce I moved from my large home, where I used to frequently entertain, to a small apartment, where I could barely squeeze into the kitchen. One night I put on my freshly washed robe and made myself a cup of hot tea. Sitting on the sofa with my hands wrapped around the pretty teacup, I smelled the fragrant fabric softener on my robe, felt the delicate china, and breathed in the warm, sweet scent of cinnamon and oranges. Deep pleasure rushed through me and suddenly I was aware that I was happy. It was a little ironic, I thought, that I had lost my possessions, my financial security, my family, and my dreams for the future, but I was sitting there feeling good about the little things in life. I wasn't faking it; I wasn't trying hard to be content with what I had. I really was.

In that instance, the overwhelming sense of what really was important burned in my heart. In that moment I finally let go of any last longings for what I'd had. I was thrilled to know that if I could find genuine peace and joy in small pleasures, that I'd never again be a slave to longing for what I did not, or could not, have.

When we can't find enough money to pay the bills, when we see others with more than we have, when our children ask for what we cannot give, when we put on that same old tired pair of sweat pants, how do we ever come to a place of being content? Since we'll never attain perfection in this life, we never will be perfectly content, but we can come close! How? By taking our focus off of what we do not have and appreciating all that we have been given.

Take off the magnifying glasses and put on the rose-colored spectacles. Once you change your attitude, you can find a little more peace about your lack of material prosperity by taking these practical steps:

Learn to Live on a Budget—One of the most powerful tools in finding freedom from financial worry is to prepare and live on a budget, and yet most of us never have. Contrary to popular opinion, it is *not* hard. Many budget-planning tools are available from accountants or in bookstores. Even a friend with a ready knowledge of income and expenses can help set you up to live within your means and free you from worry and the stress of never quite having enough!

Share Expenses—Find others in your situation and share transportation, meal preparation, baby-sitting, and clothes.

Put Your Kids to Work—Children can increase their self-esteem by pitching in and pulling their weight. Giving kids age-appropriate chores, and not too many that they are overwhelmed, helps them feel valuable. Sometimes nothing pulls a family closer than when they stand shoulder to shoulder (or up to Mom's waist) working together through crises and difficult financial times.

Division of Property

In my first divorce I left with only my clothes, leaving all my household goods, wedding gifts, and furniture with the man who had just punched me with his fists. I didn't care. I was in shock and wanted out. Later, I replaced most of what I'd had and was glad not to have memories attached to my new belongings. I never regretted the extra money I had to spend to furnish the small but comfortable apartment I shared with a girlfriend for the next eight years.

In my second divorce I fought to keep the house I'd purchased by myself prior to the marriage, assuming that would give me financial security. In my last divorce I lost everything I'd accumulated for more than twenty years. After all the emotional ups and downs, after having and losing financial power, I know today that my only real security is my Heavenly Father's love for me and his promises to always meet my needs.

It sounds simple, but it's true.

I don't know how many divorcing women I've spoken to who have lost *hundreds* of hours of sleep, spent *thousands* of dollars in attorney fees, and gotten at least a *million* new wrinkles over fighting for property and possessions.

"But my kids need it!" No they don't. They need food, clothing, shelter, and medical treatment. Teach them to get creative, earn the money themselves, trade chores for cash, or wait until you can afford it.

"But it's not fair!" You're right, it's not. What part of life is ever fair?

The Courts

In addition to my own divorce experiences, I often serve as a pastoral mediator to divorcing couples, assisting with property division, custody, and visitation issues. I've observed that our court system, designed and intended to be as fair as possible, is often complicated, confusing, and sometimes even crooked.

Some attorneys clearly explain policies and procedures, others keep you in the dark. Your attorney may be helpful, but in the court hearing you discover your ex's attorney is even sharper. Despite the fact most lawyers and judges try their best to uphold justice, in small towns where they all know each other, it can be difficult to get a fair hearing. To help you through the legal maze, you can buy guides and workbooks to help you understand court proceedings and find support groups on the Internet. Like lots of divorced women, I've been in and out of courts over custody, visitation, and support issues so many times it would make your head spin. Like others, I've hoped in the idealism of our country's principles of justice and the protection of the family. Sometimes it works; sometimes it does not. The bottom line? If you can avoid court—do so at any cost.

If you believe you must go to court, remember you are always at the whim of an imperfect legal system, a possibly uninformed or biased judge, and the prejudices of our society as a whole. Some issues warrant a hard fight; some are not worth it. You will have to decide in your own circumstance what is in the best interest of all concerned. To the extent you can work out things with an ex-spouse, do so, even if you do not get everything you want. The cost of court is high—emotionally, physically, and financially. Someone once said, "Death is cheaper than divorce because a pine box costs only a fraction of the attorney."

Being Willing to Lose in Order to Win

The story of King Solomon, who Scripture tells us was the wisest man on earth, gives us a perfect example of how women today should approach legal matters after divorce. You know the story: A woman woke up one morning to find that another young mother who lived in her house and had a baby her child's age, had rolled over in the night, smothering her own baby. She'd risen while the other was asleep, took the live baby, and replaced it with her dead child. The two women, both claiming ownership of the live baby, ended up in the king's courtroom. Unable to prove who was the real mother, King Solomon drew his steely sword and prepared to split the baby in half.

The *real* mother never would allow her baby to be killed, so she yielded her rights to the other woman. The real mother was willing to lose in order to win (1 Kings 3:16-27).

After divorce, in the struggle over money, our goal should be to take every step necessary to get what we need, but to be smart enough to *let go, give in, and give up* the fight, which will bring death to our serenity, our joy, or our family's peace. The woman with the baby got her child back by letting go. Sometimes we won't get our baby back in this lifetime, but God's promise for us is the same. Just how do we get to that place of being willing to lose in order to win?

You already know. Calm your emotions and go back to what you know in your head. *Take his hand and replace your fear with faith.*

*W*hat Does My Fear Say?

I'm afraid of losing forever what I once owned. I'm afraid my children always will be without the things they want, and that I want for them. I'm afraid I will get no justice through the courts. It's not fair, and I'm angry and scared.

*W*hat Does My Faith Say?

I can choose to be enslaved by my circumstances or freed by my attitude. I know God can send me the healing grace to help me be content with nothing, and then I'll have everything!

Love Letter

PRECIOUS DAUGHTER,

Fix your eyes on me. I will send you clarity, comfort, and counsel through others in the world, but you never will find it totally in your community. The perfection you seek from the church you can find only in my arms.

Your Loving Father

❧ 24 ❧

The Church

"Ladies, the next four years at The Loretto High School for Girls will be the best years of your lives!"

Our high school principal droned on during the orientation meeting as I fidgeted in my seat. At thirteen, I was a pimply-faced freshman sitting in a new blue uniform and wondering how I could roll my skirt up shorter without getting caught. After all, it was the sixties when miniskirts were in, speech was free, and we were supposed to be making love, not war.

As it turned out, the next four years were wonderful. In addition to high scholastic training and a wide exposure to literature, music, and the arts, I made lifetime friends whom I still see at reunions, I learned to drive a '67 Mustang stick-shift in the school parking lot, and sewed my first prom dress. As a senior, I ran for class vice president and lost, but was voted by my classmates as "Best Loved."

It's been a long time since high school, but I remember there were times, and people, who were not so good. Some teachers shamed me in front of my peers. I felt rejection when the skinny, blonde cheerleaders snubbed me. And I was not accepted, understood, or forgiven when I failed. Sometimes I had to follow what seemed like rigid rules (such as no talking or smoking in the restrooms) and ridiculous rituals (like standing, sitting, and raising our hands). At times I wanted to belong, and at times I couldn't wait to graduate!

In the school's front hall, a picture of the foundress hung in a gold filigree frame. Whenever we girls were in trouble and sitting in the principal's office, she would point to the picture and declare sternly that if the foundress could see what had happened to her school she'd roll over in her grave.

I think that the church today is not much different from my old high school. If the Founder was still in his grave, seeing what we have become might make him roll over, too!

The Church Was Never Perfect

In our naiveté, we sometimes feel hurt and angry when our churches fail us after divorce. When will we grow up and realize that, despite the original mission statement, despite the intent of the Founder, the church never will be a place of perfection of any kind? As long as humans are part of any institution, be it a school, our government, or the church, there will be both good and bad times, good and bad people. Sometimes we will alternately want to belong and to run away.

What we often look for in our church can be compared to the environment one counselor tries to create for his clients:

"I'm going to provide this person with the safest place on earth; I'm going to provide this person with a place where the defenses are not necessary, where the soul can be fully exposed without rejection; where no matter how this person fails, there's still cause for celebration because forgiveness is real; where whatever the failure, there's still opportunity for the person to become mentally healthy and spiritually alive because of the power of the Spirit."[1] An ideal to be sure, but sometimes hard to find.

God placed in our hearts a deep desire for a safe refuge, a place with eternal truth, justice, love, and support. What we can get only in heaven, we have tried to get at church. We continue to be shocked, mortified, and even furious when pastors chastise us, church committees railroad us, back stabbers ruin our reputations, and fellow worshippers judge us and cast us out . . . especially after divorce. Even the very first Christian church was plagued with arguments between members, competition for first place, doubt about the direction they should take, emotional abandonment at times of trouble, and even betrayal unto death. Why do we keep expecting anything different today?

Look for the Good

Of course our churches should be places where we can find clarity, comfort, and support after divorce, but it's time to get rid of unrealistic expectations. We don't benefit from clinging hard and fast to the desire for what we want, no matter how right, good, or ideal it is. We need to accept with graceful dignity that sometimes we can't find everything we need in one place.

If divorcees are rejected by their church community, most women either leave to find a more supportive group or stay and overlook the weaknesses of their congregation. When I ask women how their church has responded to them after divorce, their answers range from bitterness to relief to gratitude:

"I had been attending a church where the pastor was very stern about my having to stay in the marriage, no matter how abused I was. I left the church at the same time I left my husband. No regrets on either part." —*Cathy*

"I felt like an outcast! This was another source of my anger. I didn't belong anywhere at church. I wasn't a single and I wasn't married. One of the saddest things is I was only nineteen years old . . . I wasn't even one of the teens. I tried to get involved in the young adult ministry, but it was obvious I was some sort of freak. So I quit going altogether." —*Eva Marie*

"I felt rather betrayed at first. The church elders knew my husband had been involved in serious sexual sin and had told my husband he needed to tell me. He never did. Afterward I did talk to the preacher and felt better when he supported me. That meant a lot. My church has made me feel comfortable and at home. "—*Lori*

"Preachers told me to put my emotions on the shelf and pray more. I wanted to scream, "That's all I have done for eighteen years. I want to let the real feelings out *now*!"—*Angela*

"My church tried to be helpful, but it never felt like enough. When I was hungry, they fed me. But my daughters and I always felt like second-class citizens, not quite good enough. We were left out of a lot of things. One woman, whom I thought was a friend, told me, 'I'd invite you and your daughters over for dinner, but since you don't have a husband who would my husband visit with?' That hurt. We didn't measure up in a lot of ways because we had no dad in our family."
"About four years ago, I changed churches and this one is completely different. They have reached out and made us feel totally accepted. It's sad because, in my old church, I had been heavily involved as a teacher, leader of the children's church and choir, and part of the ladies' meetings and seminars. When I left, they were the losers."—*Julie*

"We changed churches, because our congregation was very family oriented. Our pastor was great, but he couldn't control the attitude of, or be responsible for, the people in his pews. At one time I even started a singles' ministry, but I got tired of butting my head against the women who thought I had designs on their men. That was very discouraging."—*Phyllis*

"I still get the looks, the comments. But it's not about church; it's about God. So I go, put on a brave front, and join in. It's okay now."—*Kim*

"Because I'm a church worker, I was careful about what I said about the divorce and to whom. I talked with my pastor and many church friends and sought out a godly counselor. I appreciate that they did not arbitrarily take sides. They even asked me lots of questions to make sure I was being fair in my story. They all have been very supportive."—*Karen*

"My church was excellent. The pastor had been through a divorce and understood the pain that affects everyone involved. In fact, he had started one of the largest singles organizations in the country, almost losing his job over it, but thankfully the church kept him and allowed him to minister to the broken hearts of the singles in our city."—*Darcy*

"My church was wonderful. The pastor's father had left his mother when he was young, and he has a special place in his heart for families affected by divorce. Although our denomination in general has a hard time with the concept of divorce, my pastor has shown nothing but the same love as God the Father."—*Veronica*

"I'm just grateful that I had my church family, because my real family left me out in the cold! I know that some people at church don't know what to think about me, but that's their problem. Most of them have been loving and kind and have bent over backward to include me in everything."—*Betty*

Focusing on Others

There's no doubt we need some support from our churches. We can find great healing in community, counseling, shared worship, financial and emotional support, and a sense of interdependence. God taught me a lesson in the middle of my divorce recovery, however, that gave me an even broader perspective of my relationship with the church community.

Like the women in Phyllis' church, some of the older women in my church initially did not offer much sympathy. I realized later that many of them assumed that once my husband left, I embarked on a mission to steal their men. I was even excluded from the church's annual volunteer Christmas party because the women who organized it thought I was playing hanky-panky with our pastor!

One woman from my church, whom I barely knew, approached me in a local restaurant and asked me to go to the restroom with her. When I did, she confronted me with her suspicions that I was having an affair with her husband. Although nothing could be further from the truth, I was healed enough not to retaliate in anger or to be defensive. Instead, I looked past the attack and saw her own pain and insecurity. I thought how difficult it must be to live with a man you think you cannot trust. Sure enough, as I reached out and took her hand in mine to reassure her, she began to cry and confessed he had been unfaithful in the past. I spent the rest of the time listening to her, meeting her emotional needs, and ended up giving a motherly hug to this woman who was old enough to be *my* mother! She and I now have a special smile for each other when we see each other at church each week.

I realized her angry attack was not at all about me . . . it was about her. It was about a woman just like me; a woman who has hurts, fears, worries, prejudices, and anxieties. Even in the midst of our own pain and suffering, God often calls us to minister to his other daughters, and in that act of coming out of ourselves, we receive the best medicine for our own emotional ailments. No matter the situation in our churches, we need to remember that when people push us away, they are hurting too and may need a hug more than we do.

When We Are Looking for Allies

One reason we might turn to a church for support is to find someone—anyone—who will validate our divorce. When I filed for the divorce from my second husband, I wanted everyone to find me blameless. I remember talking long hours with my pastor about my husband's failures and how our marriage just wasn't going to work. I was relieved when my pastor agreed with me. In retrospect, I know my husband wasn't a bad man, and I could have done things that might have saved the marriage. But my pastor assumed I had done everything possible, and I didn't tell him differently. Having my church family support my decision to leave was comforting, but it also made it easier for me to discount my part in the failed marriage.

Some women leave their husbands because they fell out of love or their needs haven't been met for a long time. Some see divorce as the only answer out of a frustrating situation, but, looking back, feel guilty about their decision. A healthy church community should hold each partner accountable for his or her actions and responses and help them embrace failures as a step toward emotional maturity. If the church body can help us face our fears, admit our failures, and come into the presence of a loving and forgiving God, then they will richly bless us.

The Good, the Bad, and the Beautiful!

Despite the bad things that happened to me, the four years I spent in high school were filled with warm, loving support from teachers who cared deeply about my personal development. They provided spiritual leadership, grace-filled role modeling, and, above all, encouraged me daily in my walk with my Heavenly Father. There was good, there was bad, but most importantly there was a chance to begin to become the beautiful woman God meant for me to be, inside and out. The churches I have attended have been the same. Maybe we find what we are looking for, or expect to see, and maybe we do not. But sometimes—not always—we need to stay and help improve a church instead of running to find a new one. Our relationship with our church family might be a little like marriage: do we run or do we stay and work it out?

What Does My Fear Say?

I'm afraid others will reject me, judge me, condemn me, or shame me. I am afraid I won't be able to find a special, warm, loving church family, or the guidance and support I need.

What Does My Faith Say?

I have choices. If I am not getting what I need from my church, I can trust God to show me another place, or I can ask for the grace to overlook the weaknesses and focus on the strengths. I will choose to take what I can, be grateful for the help, and, when I am able, give in return.

Empowering New Practices

Love Letter

My Child,

How I long for you to trust me! If you will lean on me, I will send you all the grace you need to keep your fears and worries under control. As for those who thwart you, do you not know that in the end I will bring everything under my sovereign control?

Your Loving Father

25

What You Can and Can't Control

*P*atricia stood in the aisles of the neighborhood Blockbuster store, reading the back of a videotape, when her seven-year-old daughter, Debbie, ran up excitedly and said, "Mom! Can we get this one?"

Patricia looked down absentmindedly and said, "Maybe, honey . . ." and kept reading the video she held in her hand. "Mom, *can we*? It's really good! I watched it with Daddy and his girlfriend last week."

The mention of her ex-husband made Patricia stop and take a better look at the video her daughter was thrusting up in her face. When she turned it over to read the title she almost fainted! *Pulp Fiction*, rated R, had violence, nudity, aberrant sexual themes, drugs, death, and foul language.

"You watched this movie at Daddy's?!" Patricia's angry voice screeched as her daughter shrank in fear and customers everywhere turned to see who was yelling. Tight-chested and red-faced, a fuming Patricia grabbed her daughter's hand, threw the video back on the shelf, and left the store. As she shifted the car into reverse and pulled out of the parking lot, Patricia glanced in the rear-view mirror and saw little Debbie sitting quietly in the back seat with tears welling up in her eyes. Patricia pulled back into the parking space, turned off the engine, and told her daughter to come up to the front seat for a minute.

"Honey, I'm really sorry I yelled in the store. I'm not angry with you. I'm angry with your father for letting you see that video."

"I know, Mommy, but you're always mad at Daddy."

Patricia sighed. She knew her daughter was right. Jim was irresponsible and apparently had no idea of the damage he was doing to his daughter. If he was aware, it was even worse, because he did it anyway. Patricia was frustrated because she wanted only the best for her baby, but legally she had no authority over what went on in her ex-husband's home. She was tired of being angry and feeling out of control.

Why We're Always Angry

Millions of divorced moms are stuck in the cycle of fear, anger, and bitterness, and maybe even depression, because through divorce they lost a lot of control over their schedules, their lives, and their children. In divorce, the natural and civil rights we have as parents are sharply divided.

Unfortunately, we cannot completely protect our children when they are away from us. As harsh as that reality is, we will be better mothers when we (a) do what we can, (b) grieve the loss, (c) accept reality, and (d) put our trust in God.

Most often our "control" is an illusion. We may think we control the children's bedtime, but in reality they have a free will and are choosing to obey for fear of discipline or to please. We simply create the circumstance that will help narrow their choices, or put pressure on them to make what we think is the right one. When others make choices with which we disagree, we feel out of control and we get angry. When we hold on to the anger, we become bitter; when we hold it inside we become depressed. In both instances, we need to either forgive or to be forgiven for our own attitude.

To help you avoid this cycle, you can take the following steps:

1. Identify all the areas which you can and can't control. Write them down.
2. Stop focusing on areas you can't control, and grieve the loss.
3. Start appreciating areas you can control.
4. Remind yourself about the bigger picture and ask for God's help.

What You Can't Control

Anything That Goes On in His Home. Unless something is illegal, you have no control. Document and report to authorities any illegal actions or breaches of the divorce or visitation agreement. With dates, times, places, and facts, the courts will be better able to advise and support you. Realize, though, that overburdened courts will not come alongside you in what they see as minor matters.

Anything He Says to the Kids. Even if the court agreement states there should be no parental alienation, you cannot stop another parent from saying bad things about you, your lifestyle, your morals, or your choices. Instead of focusing on what you can't control, focus on keeping open communication with your kids. Turn negative comments into teaching opportunities.

Anything He Does with the Kids. No matter where he goes, what movies he lets them see, who he visits, who visits or sleeps at his house, if it's not illegal, you can't control it. Stay focused on it and stay angry, or let go and find peace.

Anything He Gives the Kids. You have no control over whether he spoils them, gives them inappropriate gifts, lets them eat junk food at every meal, or let's them sip his beer. He can choose their books, television, and computer activity. You can, however, teach the children why it is important for them to say, "No thanks, Dad." Keep talking to and encouraging the kids without trashing their father. As they get older, they may find it easier to make their own choices when they are with him.

What He Lets the Kids Wear or How He Dresses Them. Although you may know the importance of good grooming, clothing is one of the least important issues in parenting. You can't control where he gets their hair cut, what they wear, how clean it is, how often they bathe or brush their teeth, or what time they go to bed. Be thankful that you have the authority to set standards in your own home.

What Doctor or Counselor He Lets Them See. If you have joint legal custody, the children's father can take them to whatever lessons, classes, doctor, dentist, or therapist he chooses. Unless there is clear and documented abuse, the courts are unlikely to support your objections. Talk to your attorney. If you don't have an attorney, many will provide a short-term hourly consultation.

What Church They Attend. Except in rare cases, both parents have the full rights to take their children to whatever house of worship they choose. Teach your children as much as you can about your own faith, and listen carefully when they talk about their dad's or theirs.

Where They Sleep. It's not uncommon for hurting divorced parents to want extra affection from their children. Even adult fathers can feel insecure and lonely. Make sure the children, even babies and toddlers, have a separate bed at his home. Sometimes sleeping with Daddy can be not only an emotional retardant, but also an unhealthy sexual and psychological influence, for boys and girls. If you ever suspect any inappropriate touching, adult-child bonding, or abuse, don't hesitate to get professional help.

What Companions He Lets Them Have. As children mature, their peers are often the biggest positive or negative influence. If your ex-husband does not make wise choices in monitoring his children's playmates, talk to the children and get outside counseling if necessary.

How Well He Follows the Visitation Agreement. You have no control over whether or not he's late, early, on time, or even shows at all. If he repeatedly violates the court order, you will have to choose whether to take him back to court, get creative in finding another solution, or accept the situation and let go. Nagging, threatening, yelling, begging, pleading, or giving him his own copy of your favorite parenting book probably will not work. His outward behavior is just a symptom of deeper inward attitudes. You are not his counselor. Let go.

What You Can Control

If you are a primary influence in your children's lives, you have cause for celebration! Develop a grateful attitude for what you can control at your house:

What time the children get to bed
What they eat, where they play, what they watch on TV
What they wear while they are with you
Where they go and whom they're with (except where court orders prohibit)
Their discipline and teaching in your home
Their religious and spiritual upbringing in your home
Their supplemental education, such as music, dance, art, and sports
Where you take them on vacation
Your visits to their school and conferences with their teachers
Your communication with doctors, dentists, and counselors
How often they see your friends and relatives
What toys they have in your home
Their allowance and chore schedules at home
What they learn about life, love, and God in your home

Let Life Teach Your Children. When they are upset or hurt that Dad did not show up, listen and talk to them about their feelings, and teach them how to communicate with their father in a healthy way. Share about how God has helped *you* deal with disappointments.

Do a little soul-searching and see if you might have let them down or shut the door on their feelings in any area. Have you hurt them or made them angry lately? Did they feel out of control, too?

Discuss anger and bitterness and how they keep us stuck in pain. Lead them through a grieving process. Show them what they are learning is preparing them for adult relationships and children of their own. Explain that the goal of life is not to be happy, but to become the person God wants them to be and to love others even when they feel out of control.

Remember, your children were not given *to you*, they are only passing *through you* on their way to adulthood.

What Does My Fear Say?

I'm afraid that bad things will happen if I can't control the outcome, and I'm angry and depressed about that.

What Does My Faith Say?

I keep forgetting that my Father is in control! I will keep reminding myself that I can't control my ex, but I can control my own actions and attitude.

Love Letter

DEAR ONE,

Like a city whose walls are broken down is a woman who cannot set and enforce boundaries. I have given you charge over your life. I want you to learn how to stand guard and keep safe yourself and the children within your walls. As my daughter you have inherited full authority to keep peace within your home.

Your Loving Father

❧ 26 ❧

Boundaries

id you see the movie *Jurassic Park?* On the mist-shrouded island in the middle of the Pacific Ocean, scientists were secretly breeding ferocious dinosaurs, including the terrible tyrannosaurus rex. The only thing that kept the islanders safe from the ravenous monster was a tall cyclone mesh fence. Not very formidable in structure, the wire nevertheless very effectively kept the hungry carnivores at bay. Why? Because a powerful electric current ran through the fence, and any time a dinosaur decided to push, he was zapped!

About halfway through the movie, the worst happened: the power went out on the island and the T-Rex effortlessly knocked down the fence and started gobbling up the scientists! This movie scene clearly illustrates the most important principles about boundaries, the tool we use to keep our lives in order.

Boundaries Are Necessary to Take Control of Your Life. Dr. Henry Cloud and Dr. John Townsend, authors of *Boundaries,* a series of books, cassette tapes, and videos, advise learning "when to say yes, and when to say no"[1] in order to take control of our lives. After divorce some women have trouble saying no to the demands of their ex-husband, children, friends, family, and even the church group who wants them to join one more Bible study. Healing from the heartbreak of divorce takes time and requires tremendous energy. One of the most important tools you need to get through the full recovery process is learning to say no. Realize that you can set limits in your life and still be a loving person.

Healthy Boundaries are Necessary for Protection. Boundaries bring order out of chaos and safety in times of danger. They can protect us from negative influences that make us feel hurt, used, violated, angry, out of control, fearful, or bitter. If we find ourselves caught up in a pattern of these feelings in our relationships, it's probably because we have failed to establish and maintain healthy emotional boundaries. We can protect ourselves or stay stuck in the victim role. If your ex-husband yells at you on the phone, you can continue to be abused or politely hang up and talk later. If your children push you to buy them everything, you can either learn to lovingly say no or let them continue to eat you alive with their demands. When that happens, they become self-centered and indulgent; we become weary and bitter.

Boundaries Allow Us to Be Safe Anywhere. With the fence in place, the islanders in Jurassic Park did not have to stay far away or isolate themselves, but could coexist side by side with dangerous creatures. When other people violate our rights, harm us, or take advantage of us, we often are tempted to run or avoid them. While sometimes that is possible and even desirable, we can't always refuse to see or communicate with ex-spouses or others if we share custody and visitation. When we need to talk about the children, pick them up, or make arrangements for their care, we can "coexist" with their father if we have safe, strong boundaries. The fences we erect to protect our mental and emotional well-being help us do a better parenting job and are therefore as necessary as any other way we safeguard our children.

It's Not the Boundary That Keeps the Intruder Out; It's the Consequence. The fence in the movie was flimsy. It was the consequence of overstepping the boundary (the electric shock) that made the boundary effective. Telling your children that their bedtime is 9:00 p.m. is a weak and useless boundary unless they feel a sting when they fail to go to bed on time. Telling an ex-husband he'd better be on time is another useless boundary unless you have the authority and are willing to back it up with a consequence. If you're going to be late for lunch with your mother because he hasn't shown up to take the kids, take the children with you and leave him a note telling him he needs to pick them up at the restaurant. Don't linger another half an hour, making your mother wait for you. It's not fair and only makes everyone angry. The person who violated the boundary should pay the consequence.

Boundaries Don't Have to Be Three-Foot Thick Steel Walls. Sometimes we put up huge walls because we don't trust that we are strong enough to keep someone from hurting us. That usually means we haven't (a) accepted our full rights and authority over a situation and (b) are more fearful of our own weakness in keeping them at a safe distance, or (c) simply have never learned other options. An ex-wife who completely refuses to talk to her ex-husband has erected a giant wall of protection because she doesn't know how to stand up for herself in a conversation.

When we don't see or love ourselves the same way God does, we might feel unworthy of taking charge of our own lives. We sometimes mistake firm boundaries for being cold, cruel, and unchristian. When that happens, the root issue is a fear of rejection for our behavior, either by others, the church, or God himself. We are telling God that what others think about us is more important than what *he* thinks, or that we are not precious enough to warrant loving care.

Residual guilt (false or genuine) also might keep us from feeling we have the right to enforce a boundary. Many of us feel okay about setting a limit, we are just afraid to back it up. Passive, quiet personalities have a particularly difficult time enforcing boundaries because they perceive conflict will result.

Boundaries Sometimes Invite Escalated Attack. Pit bulls and rott-weilers are known to be so enraged at times that they will charge a barbed wire or electric fence over and over despite the pain. These crazy animals often end up killing themselves. People sometimes do the same thing. Children will scream even louder when you say no, and teenagers will take the car anyway. That's the time to stand even firmer, never giving in to their increased pressure. If you do, you teach them it's okay to push harder and harder each time.

Boundaries Are Only as Strong as Their Weakest Spot. In Jurassic Park the velociraptors slowly and methodically searched every foot of the electric fence for a weak spot. People who use us or take advantage of us do the same. They find where we still feel weak, insecure, or guilty and use that to sneak past our fences. The classic example is the tantrum in the grocery store. Many mothers fear what other people will think if they take charge of their child in public. Sometimes they hate to say no too many times because their own parent was overly restrictive and they bend over backward the other way with their own kids. In any case, an emotional weak spot of fear or guilt helps make it easier to give in and give up—and the child knows it! Failing to enforce a boundary often teaches the attacker that he/she has permission to do it again, and they will.

Boundaries Show Love and Respect for Ourselves. If we are to love ourselves as we love others, we must protect ourselves as well as others. Self-care is a healthy form of loving ourselves. Refusing to be abused verbally, emotionally, physically, or otherwise is a sign that we honor and respect the way God made us and who we are.

Enforcing Boundaries Is an Act of Love to Others. Boundaries keep both sides safe. When we let others harm us, or overstep a bound-ary that would bring them harm, we encourage them to continue being selfish and sinful. When we say no, we give them the message that we care enough about them to refuse participation in any level of harm that would result from their action. If a pit bull crossed our property line and attacked our babies, we'd have to shoot him. Erecting a strong fence would safeguard the dog as well as our children, just as healthy boundaries can protect both parties.

Boundaries in Action

The following example might seem like a little thing, but it is so typical between divorced parents, it's almost a classic:

Dennis and Cathy share physical custody of their two children, Leah and Billy. When the children are with their father, their bedtime is 8:00 p.m. Dennis has asked Cathy to call the children in plenty of time before they go to bed so he can get them down to sleep. Cathy, a powerful and assertive ex-wife, knows how to push easy-going Dennis' buttons. She calls whenever she wants, often as late as 8:30, when the kids are settled in bed, because she knows Dennis will back down. Dennis told me, "I let her get away with it a few times because I didn't want to feel like a mean, controlling parent who kept the kids away from their mother (feeling unworthy). I didn't want the kids to be mad at me (fear of rejection). I also didn't want to hear her usual snotty attack if I asked her to please call earlier (fear of conflict).

"Tonight she called right at 8:00. I asked her again to please call before 8:00 (useless boundary) and she got technical on me, saying it was exactly 8:00. Whatever (giving up). She then asked if I had a problem with it (Mom pushes the fence down). I said yes, the kids were already in bed . . . but, then I went ahead and called the kids to the phone. She needs to control everything. It makes me angry, but I guess I'm just tired and coming down with a cold (stuffing the anger inward, making excuses). I'll feel better tomorrow (mythical thinking)."

Can you see how lack of self-love, failure to take authority, and fear of rejection set parents up to have useless boundaries? Their anger, a normal response, is either shot back in attack or shoved down inside, perpetuating the rejection connection between them.

I told Dennis not to blame his wife because, by backing down, he'd given her permission to ignore any boundaries he'd set. Powerful personalities usually have no trouble in setting, enforcing, and cramming their boundaries down your throat. In dysfunctional relationships the powerful personality does the pushing and the peaceful personality backs down. When peacefuls don't know how to set boundaries, they respond by stuffing it all in until one day it explodes in rage. In wanting to avoid the rage, peaceful personalities actually contribute to its build-up and inevitable damage.

After we talked, Dennis decided he would make some new rules that all parents could use in keeping the dinosaurs on the other side of the island:

1. If you can't enforce a boundary, don't set it. It only makes you angry and causes you to be bitter.
2. Backing down reinforces the abusive behavior.
3. Backing down teaches the observing children how to push to get their own way, or how to grow up to be victims themselves.
4. If Mom calls before 8:00 p.m., no matter where they are, Dad should get them to the phone, setting a time limit of five minutes to say good-night. Earlier calls can last longer.
5. If Mom calls after 8:00 p.m., Dad will say, "The kids are in bed but I will have them call you in the morning before they go to school."
6. If Mom yells and tries to engage Dad in an argument, he will say, "I hear you, but I need to go now. I'll get back to you later." That way he validates her emotions (I hear you) and sets a boundary (I need to go, because if I stay I will yell back or stuff my anger). When he says, "I'll get back to you later," he also takes the loving lead in offering a way to work with her on reconciling the situation.

What Does My Fear Say?

I'm afraid that my child will think I'm mean. I'm afraid they will want to be with their father more if I don't give them what they want. I'm afraid they might even love him more. I want to be the better parent in their eyes.

I'm worried about how I might look to others. I'm afraid of not being kind, good, or loving enough. I don't want to be a cold, harsh disciplinarian, so I find myself being the victim. I can't stop!

What Does My Faith Say?

I can stop seeking approval and acceptance from others, even my children. I know I'm totally accepted by my Heavenly Father. He has given me a responsibility to protect and care for not only my children but also myself. Instead of worrying about how I look or fearing conflict, I will learn to say no and not feel guilty.

Love Letter

MY DAUGHTER,

Consider it pure joy when life's problems plague you. I will send you the grace to pass the test of your faith and to develop perseverance. I want that for you so you can become beautifully complete, mature in grace and wisdom.

Your Loving Father

27

Problem Solving

The visitation agreement is often a primary source of problems for women who are trying to heal from divorce. Let me share an example:

Shawna had remarried four years after her divorce. She and her new husband lived with her two boys and his daughter in a new home. Her ex-husband, Jim, an irresponsible playboy type, lived two streets over because, as part of the settlement agreement, Shawna insisted he live close enough to see the boys regularly. Because she did not want to restrict the boys from their father, she gave Jim free and open access to their home any time he wanted to see the children.

Although it sounded fair and loving for all concerned, this open arrangement had major problems.

First, the boys never knew when Dad would come to visit. Because Dad knew he could visit any time, he began to be irresponsible about showing up on time, and he missed some of the boys' school programs and other events. This left the children with a sense of insecurity and a lack of trust in their father.

Secondly, When Jim arrived unannounced or at short notice for dinner or a visit, Shawna did not want to turn him away, as she thought that would be rude and even hurtful to the boys. After all, he was their father. So she changed their plans. The boys were late for friends' birthday parties, she canceled a movie with the boys' cousins, and once Shawna even canceled dinner with her parents because Jim had shown up and wanted to visit. By changing her schedule to suit Jim's visits, Shawna was inconsiderate of other people's plans.

Thirdly, when Jim came for dinner and sat around the table as a "family" with his ex-wife, Shawna and Jim gave a mixed message to their sons about the possibility of their getting back together. Although the boys never said anything, they were often whiny and argumentative, which Shawna attributed to lack of sleep.

Fourthly, Shawna's new husband, Mike, went along with the program, but deeply resented the sporadic intrusion into their private family time. Both Jim and Mike were peaceful personalities who did not know how to set boundaries, so they allowed powerful Shawna to call the shots. Mike internalized his irritation at his new wife's allowing her ex such freedom to come and go, but quickly found the subject was taboo.

Finally, because Shawna allowed Jim to continue functioning in such an irresponsible manner, he never learned to be considerate of their schedule.

As this open visitation continued, Shawna wasn't happy, the boys weren't happy, and her new husband wasn't happy. Symptoms of this lack of healthy boundaries showed up in sharp exchanges between Shawna and Jim, and Shawna and Mike; bedwetting in one of the boys; and acting up at home, in school, and with others. While Jim came and went at will, Shawna's family was plagued with lack of respect, lack of trust, insecurity, confusion, frustration, anger, and bitterness.

The Problem-Solving Technique

This five-step process can be applied to not only divorce-related problems, but also any problem. Let's see how Shawna used this technique to solve the conflict in her new family:

Admit the Problem. Admitting there's trouble brings us out of denial and into the solution stage. After we acknowledge the issue, we need to ask, "What part have I played in this?" This includes identifying the emotional roots that keep us locked in. After carefully examining the situation, Shawna shared, "I was afraid of being a bad ex-wife. I didn't want anyone to think I was being mean to Jim. I also was afraid the boys would be mad at me if I restricted their time with Dad. I see now that my fears of rejection led me to put my need for acceptance first, and my family, friends, and even my new husband last."

Accept the Problem. At this step, we imagine the worst that could happen. That primes our emotions to face our fears and put our trust back in God. It's a minicourse in working through the grieving process. Shawna continued, "I knew I had to change the routine. I imagined Jim getting angry with me, and the kids crying that they could not see their dad. I also imagined my friends at church telling me I was too rigid and would hurt my boys if I imposed a new schedule on their father. I could almost feel the hurt and grieving of everyone being mad at me. Then I imagined God standing behind me, with his hand on my shoulder, as I disappointed all these people, and I heard him whisper, "They'll get over it. Do the right thing. I'm with you." It gave me courage.

Appreciate the Problem. Every problem has the opportunity to become a pearl of great wisdom in your life. Look for the character quality you lack in the situation. Shawna realized she was letting a spirit of fear keep her from setting healthy boundaries. If she could work though this problem, *courage* to stand up against others' rejection and *confidence* in her decision-making skills would be her "pearls." Shawna realized what scripture meant about considering trials to be pure joy. "As soon as I run into a problem I stop and say, 'God, I hate to say it, but thanks! Now show me what I can do.'"

Attack the Problem. Once we have admitted the issue and mentally and emotionally come to grips with the feelings that hold us back, we should take whatever steps we can to resolve the problem. Sometimes we can make great changes; sometimes we have the power to do nothing. The "Serenity Prayer" says it perfectly:

God, grant me the serenity to accept the things I cannot change, the courage to change the things I can, and the wisdom to know the difference.

We should ask ourselves: What can I do? Can I get help? What are all my options? Is it legal? Will it hurt anyone? Is it practical, affordable? What am I willing to lose? What's really worth fighting for? For each problem, we can develop the habit of listing at least two or three options instead of the initial dead-end feeling that we can do nothing!

Shawna's solution was to call an attorney and get a specific visitation schedule filed with the court. If she drafted the document herself through a paralegal service, she could keep the cost low. She told Jim she wanted a more precise schedule and asked what might work best for him. Although he came up with several excuses for shunning the inflexibility she was imposing on him, Shawna felt better knowing she'd at least invited his comments and respected his need to be consulted and heard. She also checked with her new husband, Mike, who was thrilled about her decision. Planning ahead, and anticipating Jim's typically unclear and open communication style, Shawna made sure the visitation agreement covered specific weekly schedules, holidays, birthdays, pickup times, and places.

The solution was legal, practical, and relieved the uncertainty and doubt about when and if the boys would see their father. The clear boundaries provided a sense of security and respect for everyone involved.

At first, the boys and Jim were upset when Shawna did not let him stay for dinner when he showed up one night. Instead, she let the boys visit with their dad for a few minutes and then, calling everyone to the table, said to Jim, "Good-bye, see you Friday night."

Atone. We are always called to forgiveness and reconciliation if possible. Shawna asked Jim to forgive her for letting him continue to be irresponsible. "I know you have your own issues to work out, Jim, but I want to make every effort to not make things worse for all of us. Please forgive me."

Shawna apologized to her boys, explaining that her lack of boundaries had caused a dysfunctional domino effect in the family. She took the opportunity to teach her sons about setting boundaries of their own, and how to problem solve. She also sought forgiveness from her husband, Mike, who also learned a little about standing up to make things better.

What Does My Fear Say?

I worry about problems, sometimes, until I am either stuck in anger or frozen in fear.

What Does My Faith Say?

My help comes from the Lord! I can take practical steps, based on proven principles, to find pure joy! Thank you, God, for all my problems.

Love Letter

MY CHILD,

I know it's hard sometimes, but I want you to learn to speak with love even to those who have hurt or disappointed you. Let no corrupt communication come out of your mouth except that which will encourage the other person. I can help you. Will you learn to let me fill your mouth with sweetness?

Your Loving Father

28

Communication

oreen told me a story about the woman's divorce recovery group she attended. The participants were asked to come to the front of the room where a large piece of white butcher paper was taped over a bulletin board. The ladies were invited to take markers and draw a picture of their ex-husband (and/or his mistress if he'd had an affair) on the paper. Then each person was encouraged to take turns telling the picture, out loud, just what they thought of that person. Immediately faces with horns and scribbled hair began to appear to the paper as the women chirped and chuckled at their works of art.

Doreen was a little hesitant, and just listened while the hurt and angry ex-wives spat out venomous diatribes against the men who had abandoned and betrayed them. After a few minutes the moderator passed out darts, and told the ladies to let their anger rip. Some women became even more furious and others howled with laughter as they released their emotions along with the darts. When the attack was over, the moderator walked over to the board, removed the darts, and tore down the paper. The room suddenly fell silent as every woman saw a large picture of the face of Jesus underneath, stained by the felt pen pictures and pierced by the points of the darts. No further lesson was needed.

Why We Attack with Words

When I look back and examine the times I have "let it rip" with those who hurt me, I realize (a) I was letting my emotions control me, (b) I wasn't taking the time to remember what my faith says, and (c) I usually was not armed with something else more appropriate to say. For me, the two-step solution to avoiding verbal attacks and keeping myself emotionally on track is to *slow down* and *be prepared.*

Slowing down, even by taking a long, deep breath, swallowing, or counting to two allows us to draw on the mental reservoir we have about faith, trust, and God's promises. It's not that we don't know how to align our fears back with our faith, we often just don't give ourselves time.

Being prepared means knowing what to say in any given situation so we don't have to rely on our emotional outbursts. This requires educating ourselves and planning ahead.

Even after divorce, we're in a relationship with our ex-spouse and others with whom we will have difficulty communicating. Part of our own healing process is learning not to hurt others, because we only hurt ourselves more. To keep communication healthy, use these guidelines for the three ways in which we communicate: in person, on the phone, and in letters.

Communicating in Person

Be Consistent—Make sure your body language and facial expressions are consistent with your words. We can use honeyed words or a sweet tone of voice and still send darts with our eyes.

Breathe—If your emotions become too overwhelming, learn to breathe slowly or ask that the conversation be continued later. Leave if you have to.

Bring a Friend—If in the past talking to the other person has resulted in violence or verbal attack, take another person with you. The police will accompany women who are afraid of abuse.

Back Off—If the other person is emotionally closed, don't keep talking and explaining. You get angry and he gets irritated. Just wait for a better time.

Break Out the Stationery—If the conversation is not working, continue later or write him a letter. Letters are a perfect option for communicating clearly and without emotions. They also allow the other person time to digest what you say. Letters leave a paper trail preventing misunderstandings about dates, times, or exactly what was said.

Bounce It Back—If he attacks you verbally, answer, "I refuse to receive that. I need to be respected in this conversation and, if you're not able to do that right now, we should continue this later." Don't act snotty, superior, or self-righteous. Be kind. If he continues to bait you into an argument, leave calmly and quietly.

Communicating on the Phone

Talking on the phone is more common when ex-spouses have trouble getting along in person, but it can still be a set-up for the rejection connection. Some of the following techniques work well on the phone or in person:

Role-Play—Practice with a friend or your counselor and have him or her pretend to verbally attack you, manipulate, or otherwise set you up for an argument. Practicing new healthy ways to respond helps them come automatically when you need them!

Mirror Back What They Say—"What I hear you saying is that you'd rather have a separate appointment to see the kids' teachers. Is that right?" That gives you the chance to slow down and consider what he is saying before blurting back out of your emotions. It also gives him the chance to clarify any misunderstanding and, hopefully, to get a hold of his own emotions.

Get to the Bottom Line—If you find yourself or the other person going off on tangents or around in circles, bring it to a close. "So, the bottom line is that you will not be there at 6:00 p.m. but you *will* be there at 7:00, right? See you then." If they repeat the tangential thread, bring them back again. Repeat yourself if necessary.

Not Up for Discussion—When you shut a door, you don't have to slam it. I love the following polite but healthy verbal boundary. It lets the other person know you will not be led down the path to arguments or topics that are none of his business. "I'm sorry, but (he/she/it) is not up for discussion."

Don't "Dextify"—Part of the rise in our emotions is the other person's failure to hear us, understand us, or validate us. Sometimes that is something he won't or simply just can't give us. Quit *defending, explaining, and testifying* for yourself (In other words, don't "dextify".) Stick to the facts and get to the bottom line.

Ask for a Letter—In addition to ending a frustrating conversation by offering to write a note or letter, you can ask him for the same. "I want to consider everything you have to say, but right now I'm having a hard time. Will you write it down and send me a letter/note/email, and I will get back to you in a few hours/days/weeks?" In this way you avoid arguments and still honor and respect the other person.

Use the Nonviolent Hang-up—Hanging up is the standard way to take control over a conversation. Done in anger or self-righteousness it is rude and hurts everyone. Instead, learn to see it as the grown-up version of time out, hanging up only when all other attempts fail, when you have asked for a continuation or letter, and when there is nothing more to say. Tell him courteously, "I'm going to hang up now. I'll talk to you tomorrow after work." *Do not* wait to hear his response, as tempting as it may be. If you say you are going to hang up, *do it*. Politely.

Communicating in a Letter

Writing notes helps prevent face-to-face confrontations. You don't have to see it as the coward's way out, just an alternate until you are healed enough to talk in person.

Letters are especially helpful in documenting continuing problems. Letters allow you to release your ugly emotions on paper and then clean up the letter before you deliver it. They give the other person time to digest your thoughts and prepare his own response.

When someone walks away from you or hangs up, letters are a good way to make your thoughts and desires known to that other person. Tips for keeping your letters healthy include:

Check All the "You" Statements—"You" statements are accusatory and inflammatory. Take out the blaming tone by focusing on how *you f*eel and what *you* want. Don't say, "You hurt the children and me when you fail to show up for their game." Say instead, "We all are disappointed when you don't show up."

Correct Always and Never—No one *always* hurts the kids or *never* takes responsibility. Eliminate the emotional exaggeration from your letter and your verbal communications.

Clean It Up—Imagine the court judge, the attorneys, your friends, and even God reading your letter. Delete any shaming, attacking, and cursing words.

Change the Part Where You Ask Them to Change —"I want you to show up on time from now on." "You'd better call by 8:00 p.m." These statements assume authority over the other person that you do not have. No one likes to be told what to do, and often you are only setting him up to refuse you as his way of keeping control. Instead, just tell him what you will do. "From now on, when you're late we will leave." "Whenever you call too late, I'll need to have the kids call you later." Get the focus off their behavior and back on your own.

Clarify the Consequences—Threats, warnings, and ultimatums only serve to make everyone feel controlled, out of control, or angry. Instead, learn to set your boundary *ahead of time,* as well as the consequence that will follow. "If you don't pick up the children, I won't be doing it for you. They'll have to take the bus to day care and you'll have to drive over there to get them. They close at 6:00 p.m. I just want to let you know that when parents don't show by 6:00, they call the cops." Ex-wives who have quit "cleaning up" and let their ex-spouse face the sheriff one time, report it almost always cures him of being late again. Don't worry about the kids, they'll still be safe. Your other choice is to let your ex-husband train you to continue the dance of the angry enabler.

Copy Your Letter—Copy all letters and stick them in a file. When we forget dates and times it helps to have a written reference.

Cast Off Abuse—Throw away any abusive letters you receive. Don't resort to returning them, tearing them up, or rereading them. That only serves to keep you in bondage to the other person's rejection. Whenever you get a nasty letter from someone, you'll probably have to do a quick run-through of the grieving process: shock, anger, grieving, acceptance, and letting go. When you feel the emotions rise, stop to check what your faith says.

What Does My Fear Say?

I don't want to talk to the other person because he might overpower me again or we'll end up fighting. I just don't know how to get through to him!

What Does My Faith Say?

I don't have to get through. How my communication is received is completely the other person's issue. My part is to make sure I communicate as clearly and lovingly as possible, with the focus on my attitude, not their behavior. God will make sure my needs are met.

SECTION

 V

Enoying Your Passions

Love Letter

MY PRECIOUS ONE,

Be patient. I know your time of singleness sometimes seems like a barren desert where you thirst for love, companionship, and intimacy. Remember that I know all your desires and I will meet all your deepest needs; I will send you the cool, wet rain in its season. For now, can you be content to love and be intimate with me?

Your Loving Father

❧ 29 ❧

Singleness

he weather turned cold today for the first time since last
winter. The sky was gray-white and misty. I dug out my
favorite jeans, slipped them on, and pulled a soft cotton sweater
over my head. After months of wearing shorts and T-shirts it felt
funny, but familiar at the same time. Like being single.

Similar to rotating seasons, I've been changing from single to
married to single again. This cycle is not what I ever wanted or
planned for, but here I am again. This morning as I dressed, I was
keenly aware of my current life and how far away being married
seems. I know it will probably come again, like the hot summer days
of next year, but for now I am enjoying the season of singleness. Like
my warm winter wardrobe, it feels a little funny, but familiar.

After breakfast, I decided to make a big pot of hot vegetable
soup to go with the cold winter weather. When I was in the grocery
store, filling my cart with curry powder, potatoes, and cans of car-
rots, I heard the faint but friendly sound of chocolate chips calling
my name. Like magic, I was suddenly in front of the baking section. I thought, "Hey, it's Saturday. I have all day to myself, and
last year's jeans still fit. Why not go for it?" Deciding to treat myself
to a fresh batch of homemade cookies, I grabbed the semisweet
chocolates off the shelf. A little farther down the aisle, I found the
nuts, who had something quite important to say to me, too.

When you're single, going all the way means splurging on the fancier pecans instead of walnuts! As I examined the clear, crisp, cellophane bags, I noticed that I had a choice of pecan pieces or whole pecans. You might call *me* nuts, but that's when the pecans began to talk to me, saying "Rose, you got pretty chopped up in your divorce, but you're not alone. This shelf is like the world, piled high with divorced women; some will end up permanently broken and some will be whole again. Which do *you* want to be?"

One Flesh

In recovering after divorce, I didn't need Scripture to remind me that I had become one flesh with my husband. The excruciating pain told me I was no longer whole. Any woman who has lived with, loved, and had children with a man knows that not only do you become one in the physical act of love, you bond mentally and emotionally as well. I had learned that my mind and emotions were just as much a part of my flesh (everything that makes us human) as the part that fit in my favorite jeans.

The divorce caused a terrible, deep tearing apart, not a clean cut. Marriage was like the smooth, shiny pecan shell that held the two halves together, and when we cracked into pieces, parts of me went with my husband, and parts of him stay stuck with me. After divorce we were not whole; we were both broken.

I looked at the price of the whole pecans. They were much more expensive than the broken pieces. Whole nuts are much more pleasing to the eye, as anyone who has made cookies or pies can attest. We always put the perfectly whole pecans on the top of the pie, or in the middle of the cookie, because they are the most desirable.

Standing in the store, I was overcome with a deep appreciation for this time in my life when I am becoming whole again, something I know God desires for me. No matter what he has planned for my future, I don't want to bring any brokenness to a relationship, whether with a friend or lover. I want others to find in me a value that's twice the price of the other nuts!

Singleness Means Wholeness

Dr. Myles Munroe, the author of *Single, Married, Separated and Life After Divorce,* is one of my favorite guest speakers on the DivorceCare videos. His message to divorced men and women is clear: singleness is not brokenness. Dr. Munroe teaches that as singles we are to be "separate, unique, and whole." Look at what Webster says about those three words:

Separate: set apart from others; distinct

Unique: unmatched; unequaled; rare

Whole: In a healthy state, sound; well; restored to a sound state; healed; not broken or fractured; not defective or imperfect; entire; complete; intact; a thing complete in itself.

Wow! I like to think that as a single I am all those wonderful things. As a single I am distinct, unequaled, and perfect . . . sounds a little like a rare and brilliant gem to me! Too often we buy into the false message that society, our friends, family, or church says about the stigma of being single. Forget that you don't "fit" . . . instead, understand you are unique.

To make the most of our season of singleness, we can take these steps:

- Remember that this time in your life is a season, not eternity.
- If you struggle with loneliness and isolation in your singlehood, God can meet those emotional needs in various ways, not just through a new romantic relationship.
- No one is ever perfectly content. God saves that for heaven!
- Use this time to become the most beautiful you can be, inside and out. Then if God blesses you with someone new, you will be ready!
- If you're really brave, call up your ex-spouse and ask him what parts of you bothered him the most. Tell him you want to hear it all, and then listen. After getting yourself emotionally back in the arms of your Heavenly Father, you'll probably want to start working on these areas.

- Don't limit yourself to one kind of growth or change. Make a list of what you can do to develop physically, mentally, emotionally, and spiritually.
- Start a new love relationship with whomever God may have for you in the future. Just because you don't know who he is, doesn't mean you can't write him a love letter. Tell him how you are feeling right now and what you hope for the future. Save the letters for him.
- Use this time to reach out to others. If you have young children, most of your time is taken trying to successfully be a single parent, and that is your most important, or maybe only, service. For older divorcées or those without kids, find an area where you can share your natural gifts and talents, so that the volunteer time doesn't seem like a penance. Remember to be a cheerful giver and get off the train if you're on a performance trip.
- Pick a passion you've put on the shelf for awhile. Take it down, dust it off, and go for it!
- Remember you're still healing. Take it easy and get lots of rest. Give yourself permission to spoil yourself silly once in awhile.
- Trust God whenever you feel bad about being single. He has a plan for you.
- Thank God every day for the gift of singleness, because through it he can give you pearls of not only great wisdom, but of peace.

God's Recipe for Singles

Little Andrea came into the kitchen and asked her grandmother for something yummy. Grandma asked her if she wanted to eat some raw eggs.

"Yuck, no! Grandma!" said Andrea, her nose wrinkling in disgust.

"What about some vegetable shortening?" asked Grandma.

"No way!" replied Andrea.

"Flour? Salt? How about a big bite of baking soda?"

"Grandma! What is wrong with you?" Andrea asked. "Don't you have any cookies?"

"Ahhh-hhh cookies!" Grandma smiled. "Do you want cookies?"

"Yes!" Andrea beamed.

"Well, first you have to mix all those ingredients and bake them, and then you will have exactly what you want! God is like that with us," explained Grandma. As Andrea listened, Grandma began to lay the ingredients on the counter.

"To make our lives delicious, he takes all the things in our life that seems yucky, mixes them together, and lets us feel the heat. When it's *just the right time*, he will take us out of the oven."

Singleness also has distasteful elements (like single parenting, lack of time, too much time, poverty, and loneliness), yet God can bring them all together to create something delicious. And while the heat feels uncomfortable, God knows exactly how long to keep you in it. When will your life be different? When will you have a new love, a new life, or a new passion? *When it's just the right time.*

What Does My Fear Say?

I'm not happy with the way things are. Oh, I can spend time with the kids or friends, and usually I am satisfied, but sometimes I ache for loving arms, and I think they may never come. At times I think I need only the children, but the thought creeps into my mind, "What will it be like when they grow up and move out?" I don't like to think of that.

What Does My Faith Say?

If I have to say it to myself a million times, I will: God does know my needs, he does promise to meet them, he does love me and want the best for me. He promises me all these things, and I will believe him. Summer will be here before I know it.

Love Letter

MY PRECIOUS ONE,

You are worth your weight in gold. You're worth more than many sparrows, and far more than rubies. Don't devalue yourself by rushing into more pain. Won't you take heart and wait for me? I know what you need, and I will deliver.

Your Loving Father

30

Dating and Sex

I'd started dating a man who used to be my neighbor and was known around town to be a really nice guy. He was. Bob was tall and handsome, with a good job, a cute little house, two sons, and a family dog. I felt at home with Bob, because we had the same philosophies on life, liked the same music, shared similar passions, and both loved Mexican food. At first I just wanted to be friends, but he worked hard at sweeping me off my feet. He sent me flowers, brought me candy, and told me everything my ex-husband never told me: "I'll never leave you." . . . "I'd do anything for you." . . . "I'd give up my dream for you." And he said the three little words all women long to hear, "You're not fat!" That did it. I fell in love.

A funny thing happened after that. As soon as I let him catch me, he began to back off. Six years earlier he'd survived a bitter divorce that left him almost penniless. Bob had worked hard to stabilize financially and plan for retirement, but he never completely healed emotionally. He'd been to counseling, but when the worst of the pain was over, he didn't want to dig any deeper. When I opened the door to talk about the "C" word (commitment), he ran for the hills. We struggled for a year in the on-again, off-again dance until he finally left for good. I was devastated.

After divorce I had been careful to open my heart ever so slowly, giving it plenty of time, hoping I could do it right this time. I see now that even though there we genuinely cared for each other, neither of us was ready. I was too eager to be loved again, and he was too afraid of being dominated, drained, and divorced one more time.

I was surprised that after dating this man just a short while, I went into a depression that lasted longer, and hurt more, than when my husband left. Why? Although I thought differently, I hadn't really completed all of my emotional healing from the divorce. Bob's rejection was like pouring salt into a freshly opened wound. Surprisingly, I also found myself angry again with my ex-husband for having thrown me, like an innocent lamb, out into a den of wolves. I couldn't blame it all on him, though. Because I didn't take the time to thoroughly assess how I would reenter the dating world, nor did I reevaluate my basic approach to relationships, I had reverted to dating the same old way and ended up with the same old pain.

How Will I Know When I'm Ready to Date?

Audrey shared advice she received about being ready to date: "Someone told me if you think you are ready for a relationship, then you need to be willing for that person to take your hand and hold it tightly as you run as fast as you can. Then, when you get to the edge of the cliff, jump as far and as hard as you can, free-falling. Ohhh, I was ready to be loved and held again, but not for *that*. A few years later, though, I was ready."

Audrey was like many of us after our divorce. We may feel ready, but we're not really ready. We may ache for company, security, and love, but our hearts still need healing. Have you ever felt better after a long, sweaty night battling the flu bug? You may wake up feeling refreshed and ravenous, but your poor stomach is not ready for solid food. Tea and toast will have to do for awhile, even though you crave a hamburger! Dating after divorce is similar; we get into trouble when we rush to McDonald's because we're not content with simple fare. Sometimes we rush because we fear that we will never have meat again. As we reintroduce foods a little at a time, dating again should start out slowly and carefully.

Are you ready to date? Before you decide, "take your temperature" in these areas:

Dating Brings Up Old Memories. Have you healed from the hurt, anger, fear, or bitterness from your old relationship? Do you still have nightmares or troubling thoughts of your ex-spouse? Milk cartons have expiration dates, but memories don't. Don't sour a new relationship with old bitterness. Continue counseling and give it a little more time. Remember: *a whole woman attracts a whole man; a wounded woman attracts a wounded man.*

Dating Brings Up Old Emotions. Do you still feel unsure of who you are, what you want in life, or where you are going? Do you mistrust men or have an addictive need to be loved? In Pia Mellody's book, *Facing Love Addiction,* she shares some practical tools to help you examine old emotions and break old patterns, thus changing the way you love.[1] Dating can distract you from answering the questions that are vital to your emotional and spiritual health. Unhealed emotions only hurt new relationships.

Dating the Same Old Way Will Get You the Same Old Men. Do you know God's way for dating? He wants us to take it slowly, ask lots of questions, pray for wisdom and discernment, establish a trusting friendship first, and save sex for marriage. Do you know how to do that? I didn't. I admit that as educated as I was, even in my forties, I had never learned to date the right way. Do the men you date know the importance of healthy dating? Becoming physically intimate too soon *blinds us* to our partner's character defects and *binds us* as one flesh, so that it's almost impossible to get out of a bad relationship. The high divorce rate for second and third marriages is attributed primarily to repeating old patterns with new people.

Dating Calls for Magnifying Glasses, Not Rose-Colored Glasses. Benjamin Franklin said we should enter marriage with our eyes wide open and afterward keep our eyes half shut. Tolerating human weakness is a strength inside marriage, but looking at someone through romantic eyes before we really get to know them can lead to another failure. Take the time to take a good, hard look, and talk about everything that is important to you. Scrutinize and analyze this person with whom you plan to entrust your heart again. Having faith in the future is different than foolish optimism.

Dating Takes Lessons and Practice. Have you ever had a sore buttocks from horseback riding? The pain comes from not knowing and practicing the proper techniques. Why do we think we can simply get back up on the horse and win the derby when we have not made the effort to educate ourselves on what we have been doing wrong all these years and practice the necessary changes to do it right? Do you know what to look for in a new romance? Do you know what questions to ask and when to ask them? Do you know how to take it slow, or how to spot red flags?

How Can I Do It God's Way?

When I talk to groups of teens, I give them a new definition of S.E.X., which works for any single person of any age:

S—*Surrender Your Will to God's Way.* Dr. Tony Evans, who ministers frequently to large singles audiences, reminds us God did all the work in putting the first couple together. Adam longed for a mate, so God, the Supreme Matchmaker, took care of everything. He did it then for Adam, he can do it now for us. Playing the romantic game and binding ourselves sexually, even when we are in love, is not God's way. He wants us to learn his way, learn about ourselves, and learn about the other person. God's way calls for instruction first, then intimacy. Are you willing to trust him to bring that special someone to you?

E—*Educate Yourself.* Hundreds of excellent books, tapes, videos, and classes show us how to communicate, honor, respect, and love each other the right way. They include tips on staying chaste, working through problems, parenting, blended family issues, and anything you want to know about having a successful relationship. What holds us back from furthering our education in relationships? Fear of facing ourselves (What if we have to change?) and of discovering flaws in others (Don't show me his faults; I want him to be "the one"). Mental and emotional laziness also keeps us stuck. We want it all to be easy, like in the fairy tales.

X—*Cross Out What the World Says.* Become aware of, and refuse to buy into, the world's messages of extreme self-absorption, self-fulfillment, self-satisfaction, and its obsession with beauty, sex, and seduction. Books, television, movies, and music all urge us to grab happiness whenever and wherever we can. Some women are afraid to embrace God's way and say no to the world because they think life will be boring, deprived, and dull, yet he offers true joy. Living a pure and holy life doesn't mean you have to start buying your clothes at the Amish thrift shop. God's daughters can be smart, savvy, and sexy and still conform to God's truth.

Dating Versus Courtship

Much has been written lately about whether or not we should date at all before marriage or remarriage. Author Josh Harris shares in his book *I Kissed Dating Goodbye*, that he chose to quit dating altogether, even refusing to kiss his girlfriend until their wedding day.[2] That worked for Josh, and certainly can be a good option for many, but it may not be for you. Regardless of how you date, it's important that you draw the line where it will keep *you* from becoming too intimate, either physically or emotionally, too soon. If you want some help in establishing healthy boundaries in dating, Jeremy Clark's *I Gave Dating a Chance*[3] offers a balanced and practical approach to doing it God's way.

Disillusioned with the high rates of divorce and broken relationships, many couples today are looking for an alternate approach to the way they have dated in the past. Courtship is one way to "date" God's way. Dating is like looking to rent, courtship is like looking to buy.

Current dating styles say, "Let's enjoy each other while we can, with no real regard to the future, because that might cramp our style. Please don't push your expectations for commitment on me right now. We can talk about that later (maybe). If it works, fine. If it doesn't, don't blame me." Dating is primarily self-centered and self-protective.

Courtship on the other hand says, "Let's get to know each other mentally and emotionally, without the false illusion of intimacy that sex introduces. I already know that sex is great, and I can wait because I want more than the flash or thrill of romance. I also know that God made us both to need true intimacy and complete trust, and I don't want to do anything that would damage that for you."

Aren't *those* the words we long to hear a man say to us?

What About the Kids?

Some women decide not to date at all until the kids are grown and out of the house. Some are overly anxious to replace the children's father and rush into dating right away. Although you have to decide what's right for you according to God's way, both of these approaches can be unhealthy extremes. Because you are trying to heal, and because more pain and confusion can result from not knowing which path to take, it's important to consider the following:

- Always have your first few dates alone and away from the children so you have enough time to discern if this man is courtship material.

- Don't discuss intimate details about your dates with the children, even if they are older. Share with a friend, a coworker, or another adult instead. Of course, you can tell the kids where you went and how much fun you had, or why you like this person. But keep it at that for now. If brought into your adult life, the children will try to become either your parent, protector, or confidante, a role that God does not intend for them.

- Don't ask your children's permission to date or marry. They are not your parents and you do not owe them accountability. When you get more serious in a relationship, you can ask the older children's opinions, letting them know what they think is important, but not final. Checking with children to get their permission only creates the false illusion that they are in control. Underneath their false sense of security, which results from you putting them first, is anxiety and anger that the adult in the house (you) is not really in charge, or leaving the children to make decisions that they really can't, and shouldn't, make.

- If you have made your children your life, expect one or more of them to act out, disapprove of, or reject your new friend. Encourage your children to express their true feelings, but never tolerate the silent treatment, snotty attitudes, anger, or tantrums. If your kids don't know how to express hurt or anger in a respectful way, begin to teach them.

Will I Ever Have Sex Again?

Having been married, we all know the excitement, pleasure, and joy of sex. God designed us as sexual beings and intended that we enjoy his gift to us within marriage. While staying chaste and remaining abstinent is his choice for us as singles, he'd never ask us to do something that was impossible. Of course it can be difficult, torturous at times, but we can take steps to keep our focus on many other pleasures in life: friends, family, food, fun, reading, music, hugs, and hobbies, and lots more.

If you want to get caught up in the exciting (but ultimately disappointing) trap of sexual preoccupation and sexual behavior outside marriage, then expect to be hurt again. If you want to wait and save sex for the richness and fullness of another marriage, change your focus in these areas:

- Stop watching racy or overly romantic movies that make you crazy for love and sex. Right after my divorce, I changed channels quickly, not out of a spirit of fear, but of knowing my emotional vulnerability.
- Quit reading romantic and sexual novels. Our focus, whether conscious or not, will be on what we watch and read.
- Don't dress to emphasize your sexual self. When I dress sexy, I feel sexy. Being divorced and struggling with the negative parts of singleness can be hard enough, why torture yourself (and others) in this area?

Women who have been on a diet understand this principle. We stay away from the tempting foods we choose not to have right now, and we replace them with something healthier. If I think about a chocolate donut long enough, I can work myself up into such a frenzy that I will stop whatever I am doing, hop in the car, and race to Winchell's. Just writing about it makes me almost taste it! So I discipline myself not to entertain the thought.

Sexual thoughts will come knocking on your door at the oddest times and places. Don't worry or be ashamed, that's normal. But don't invite them in, sit them on your sofa, and ask them to stay for tea. *That's* when you'll get into trouble.

What Does My Fear Say?

I'm so frustrated and tired of being sexually alone. Sometimes I think I'll die! It's not fair that I have to go without sex and all the closeness it brings. I worry about how long it will be before I am with a man again, if ever. Sometimes I drive myself crazy with the thoughts!

What Does My Faith Say?

I believe God knows all my needs and promises to meet them . . . even my sexual needs. I trust his grace will help me accept whatever state I am in. I expect to sometimes be content and sometimes not, because both are part of life. I can wait . . . knowing that whatever God has planned for my future it will be wonderfully, completely satisfying.

Love Letter

MY LOVE,

Stay with me now, forever. You are my beloved and I am yours. I have called you by your name. You are mine.

Your Loving Father

❧ 31 ❧

Your True Love

*L*ittle girls want Daddy's lap; grown-up girls want a lover's arms.

As children, we long for our father's leadership, protection, and love. When we mature, we wait for Romeo to arrive, Prince Charming to dance with, or our knight in shining armor to carry us off. Little boys first fall in love with their mothers. They, too, grow up dreaming of the perfect romantic partner; one who will meet their every need and come alongside them with love and support.

Our longing for love in this world reflects our desire for the perfect love of our Creator. Our loves of fathers, mothers, husbands, and wives, are pale imitations of the One True Love.

*S*eeing God as Father

Roger, who was devastated by his divorce, found emotional healing in visualizing God as his loving father. He wrote, "My separation from my wife was, like many others, very traumatic. I found that after a couple of weeks of not sleeping for more than a few minutes at a time, I was a wreck. I was depressed and torn up inside, and my nerves and body couldn't take another sleepless night. As I drifted off one evening, I remembered the DivorceCare video that said God

273

was my refuge, and underneath me were his everlasting arms. I pictured myself crawling up into his lap, laying my head on his shoulder, and cuddling in the safety and love of my Savior.

"I went right to sleep and slept for over ten hours. When I woke up I remembered climbing down from his lap and going on to have a great day!

"This might sound silly, because I am a grown man, but it may help someone else who is going through divorce. All I can say is that was one of the best night's sleep I've ever had."

Seeing God as Your Comforter

Because he gifted us with our human bodies, no one understands better than God that sometimes we need to see, hear, taste, and touch in order to "feel" his love. This story illustrates that some of us even need to talk out loud to him as we would any other loved one.

A man's daughter asked the local minister to come pray with her dying father. When the minister arrived, he found the man in bed, his head propped up by two pillows, and an empty chair beside the bed.

"I see you were expecting me," said the minister.

"No, who are you?" asked the father.

"I'm the new minister at our church. When I saw the empty chair, I assumed you knew I was coming."

"Oh, the chair . . ." said the bedridden man. "Come in, and please close the door."

The sick man motioned the minister closer and whispered, "I've never told this to anyone, not even my daughter. You see, all my life I never really knew how to pray, until a few years ago my best friend said to me 'Joe, prayer is just a simple matter of having a conversation with God. Here's what I suggest. Sit down in a chair and place an empty chair in front of you. In faith, see God in the chair across from you and just start talking. He really is with you all the time, so you should just talk to him like you would a friend.'"

The old man continued. "I know it looks kinda silly, but it works. It helps me feel like he really hears me, and I spend an hour or so every day with him that way. I'm careful, though, because if my daughter saw me talking to a chair, she'd have a fit or send me off to the funny farm."

The minister was deeply moved by the man's simple faith and encouraged him to continue his talks with God. Then he prayed with him and returned to the church.

Two nights later the daughter called the minister to tell him her father had died earlier that day.

"Did he die in peace?" asked the minister.

"Yes, before I left the house at about two o'clock, Dad called me over to his bedside, told me he loved me, and kissed my cheek. When I got back from the store an hour later I found him dead."

She continued, "But there was something strange about his death. Apparently, just before he died, Daddy leaned over and rested his head on the chair beside his bed. Why do you think he did that?"

The minister wiped a tear from his eye and said, "I wish we all could go like that."

Seeing God as Your Lover

I admit that when I first got the following email from Barb, I found myself thinking she was a little whacko. I quickly moved past my initial judgmental attitude, though, because I realized in my own divorce recovery, I, too, had taken God as my one true love. I became fascinated with her story:

"My former husband and I loved to travel, and that's something I really missed after our divorce. My ex was well-educated in history, geography, culture, and politics, and traveling with him was like having my own personal tour guide. He left me in 1996 for another woman, and I was devastated and depressed.

"About a year later, I found a new love relationship with God, understanding that only he could heal me completely and meet my needs like no husband could. I still longed for a husband someday, but in the meantime, I decided to visit the Holy Land. I began telling people I was going to Israel to visit my bridegrooms' hometown and meet his relatives. 'Oh, is he Jewish?' they'd ask, and I would tell them with a smile, 'Yes!'

"As I saved and planned for my trip, I found myself one day in a shopping mall in another town, quite by accident, where I saw a beautiful white wedding dress on sale. Now mind you, I was fifty-one years old and the thought of buying that dress had me worried about my own sanity, but I bought it anyway. I also started listening to the words of a beautiful love song that spoke of a groom's love and desire for his bride. Sometimes, when my friends came over for dinner I showed them the wedding dress and played the song. You should have seen the look on their faces!

"I finally went to Israel in 1998. We were allowed only one suitcase for the sixteen-day journey. Even though it took a lot of room, I packed the wedding dress. On the last day we visited Tiberias. I walked along the shore of the Sea of Galilee in my bridal gown. Later, in Jerusalem, I went to an archeological dig at Tel Maresha, mentioned in 2 Chronicles. I uncovered a rock about the size of a baseball, and to my amazement when I cracked it open, I discovered an intact, ancient bronze ring (dated 200–300 BC by the Israel Antiquities Authority). You see, in the midst of my painful healing from divorce, God gave me a ring, for he truly is my bridegroom. 'My beloved is mine, and I am his' (Song of Solomon 2:16, KJV)."

Knowing Him and Loving Him

After divorce some amount of healing can occur through friends, community support, and learning to change certain behaviors. But complete healing of our souls and spirits, and restoration to a place of total joy, can only come from the one who created us. Do you really know him yet?

He's strong and vibrant, powerful and perfect. He gave you life and calls you by name. He knows every inch of you, inside and out, and adores you despite your flaws. He sees in you what no one else sees, and he values you more than life itself.

He sends you flowers in the springtime and baskets of fruit in the summer. He brings you sunshine in the mornings and rainbows to let you know he is still with you even in the tough times.

He would never leave you in a rut, so he sends the change of seasons to spice up your life. When it's hot, he sends shade and cool water. When it's cold, he provides you with the heat of a fire and the comfort of warm wool.

He promises to meet your needs, dry your tears, and be your strength in time of trouble. He is the rock on which you can build your life, your home, and your family. He will be your husband. He also will be father to your children and love them more than you ever could.

He is the maker of heaven and earth. He is power and glory and might, and at his name every knee shall bend and every head shall bow.

He will never betray you or abandon you, and he will heal your broken heart.

He loves you.

He is with you always . . . even after divorce, even until the end of time.

What Does My Fear Say?

Nothing! From this day forward I will no longer give in to my fears.

What Does My Faith Say?

Everything! I feel your total, unending love for me! I will rest in you. I will feel your everlasting arms beneath me. Although my weeping may endure for the night, my joy comes in the morning! I love you, too!

Endnotes

Chapter 1
God Our Caring Parent

1. Randy Carlson, *Father Memories* (Chicago: Moody Press, 1992), 8.

Chapter 2
God As Healer

1. Dr. Tim Clinton, *Before a Bad Goodbye* (Nashville: Word Publishing, 1999), p. 39
2. Florence Littauer, *Personality Plus* (Grand Rapids: Fleming H. Revell, 1990)

Chapter 3
Loss

1. Bob Burns and Tom Whiteman, *Fresh Start Divorce Recovery Workbook* (Nashville: Thomas Nelson Publishers, 1992), 7.

Chapter 4
Shock and Denial

1. Elisabeth Kubler-Ross, *On Death and Dying* (New York: Simon & Schuster, 1969).

Chapter 5
The Rejection Connection

1. Dr. Gary Lawrence, *Rejection Junkies* (Phoenix: GLS Publishing, 1996), 111.

Chapter 6
Anger

1. Dr. Gary Chapman, *The Other Side of Love* (Chicago: Moody Press, 1999), 20.

Chapter 7
Depression

1. Dr. Les Carter, Ph.D., *The Freedom from Depression Workbook* (Nashville: Thomas Nelson Publishers, 1995), xi.

Chapter 8
Guilt

1. Using personal insights and creative license, I've expanded this story from John 4:1-42.
2. Lawrence, op. cit., 104.

Chapter 9
Fear

1. Dr. Gerald Jampolsky, *Love Is Letting Go of Fear* (Berkeley: Celestial Arts, 1979)
2. Neil Anderson, *Victory Over the Darkness* (Ventura: Regal Books, 1990), 31.

Chapter 10
Loneliness

1. Benner & Hill, *Baker Encyclopedia of Psychology and Counseling*, 2nd Ed. (Grand Rapids: Baker Books, 1999), p. 698.
2. Backstreet Boys, "Show Me the Meaning of Being Lonely," *Millennium* (Warner Brothers, 1999).

Chapter 14
Understanding the "Why"

1. Dr. James Dobson, *When God Doesn't Make Sense* (Wheaton: Tyndale House Publishing Company; 1993), 221.
2. Gary Richmond, *It's a Jungle Out There* (Eugene: Harvest House Publishers, 1996), 7.

Chapter 22
Your Kids

1. Judith Wallerstein, Julia Lewis, and Sandra Blakeslee, "Fear of Falling," *Time Magazine* (September 25, 2000), 74.
2. Ibid, 74.

Chapter 24
The Church

1. Larry Crabb, "An Interview with Larry Crabb", *Christian Counseling Today*, Vol. 8, No. 1 (Summer 2000), 36.

Chapter 26
Boundaries

1. Dr. Henry Cloud and Dr. John Townsend, *Boundaries* (Grand Rapids: Zondervan Publishing House, 1992), 27.

Chapter 30
Dating and Sex

1. Pia Mellody, *Facing Love Addiction* (New York: Harper Collins, 1992).
2. Joshua Harris, *I Kissed Dating Goodbye* (Oregon: Multnomah Books, 1997).
3. Jeremy Clark, *I Gave Dating a Chance* (Colorado Springs: Waterbrook Press, 2000).